LOVE YOUR NEIGHBOR

How Psychology Can Enliven Faith and Transform Community

Katherine M. Douglass and Brittany M. Tausen

WILLIAM B. EERDMANS PUBLISHING COMPANY
GRAND RAPIDS, MICHIGAN

Wm. B. Eerdmans Publishing Co.
2006 44th Street SE, Grand Rapids, MI 49508
www.eerdmans.com

Published 2026
Printed in the United States of America

32 31 30 29 28 27 26 1 2 3 4 5 6 7

ISBN 978-0-8028-8523-4

Library of Congress Cataloging-in-Publication Data

A catalog record for this book is available from the Library of Congress.

"This book shimmers with practical wisdom for loving our neighbors better. It invites readers to reflect on everyday life and discern concrete steps for faithful action. It doesn't just call us to love—it shows us how."

—**TED A. SMITH,** Emory University

"Written for what Martin Luther King called 'the fierce urgency of now,' *Love Your Neighbor* is a master class on integrating the inner work of spirituality with the empirical work of science for the sake of coming together in a divided world. Timely, nuanced, refreshingly practical, and blessedly compelling, *Love Your Neighbor* is your church's very next read."

—**KENDA CREASY DEAN,** Princeton Theological Seminary

"This book is needed now more than ever. In a world dominated by divisive political rhetoric, rampant greed, and uncertainty about the future, we need voices like Douglass and Tausen to take us back to the heart of the gospel. Whatever your politics, no matter your theological tradition, whether you're new to Christianity or you don't remember a time in your life when Jesus didn't matter, this book is for you. The authors will provoke, challenge, encourage, and affirm you as they stretch your imagination toward greater love for all people, even—no, wait—*especially* those who are most difficult to love."

—**DAVID M. CSINOS,** Atlantic School of Theology

"In this thoughtful and readable book, Douglass and Tausen provide both a richly researched and highly practical account of the struggle to live as good neighbors in an increasingly polarized world. The authors offer not only a diagnosis but a remedy— to seek the 'transforming of our minds' so that we may think and act in a more Christlike way with the people we meet and live alongside. This is contemporary writing on discipleship at its best, combining scientific insights with biblical scholarship to offer real-life, down-to-earth advice."

—**NICK SHEPHERD,** Church of England

"In sports, discipline and practice create results. This book shows how the same is true in faith—its exercises train us to love others with consistency and compassion."

—**D'ANTHONY SMITH,** Super Bowl champion and licensed mental health practitioner

"Douglass and Tausen's integration of social psychology and practical theology is unique and compelling. Personally honest and scientifically grounded, the book weaves together stories, data, and Scripture that stir both the mind and spirit, awakening a sense of curiosity and wonder about what's possible in our neighbor-loving when we understand the challenges and engage the tools we've been given. While the world is full of barriers to community care, this book removes those barriers, making room for deep faith transformation and more tender ways of seeing and loving our neighbors."

—**KATEY HAGE,** Seattle Quest Church

"Douglass and Tausen offer much-needed spiritual medicine for the twin epidemic of loneliness and polarizing contempt tearing through society today. Psychological principles considered theologically combined with theological convictions fleshed out psychologically propel the reader to take a risk of love toward one's neighbors."

—**GORDON S. MIKOSKI,** Princeton Theological Seminary

"Theology and psychology have been adrift from each other for far too long. Douglass and Tausen are well qualified to remedy this problem, and they do so in an invitational manner. They reunite psychology and theology in practical ways that will impact readers' relationships with their neighbors and with themselves."

—**SARAH ANN BIXLER,** Eastern Mennonite University

CONTENTS

FOREWORD

I yearn for Christian resources that equip the church to live more faithfully. Far too many discipleship materials fail to take science seriously and neglect the necessary inner work required to truly bear witness to the transformative power of the gospel of Jesus Christ in a culture obsessed with self, scarcity, and individualism.

Refreshingly, this book bucks both of those trends. In a much-needed and long-overdue innovation, it is coauthored by a practical theologian and a social cognitive psychologist—two scholars committed to equipping everyday people in their journey with Jesus. This interdisciplinary approach makes the book uniquely practical, helping us understand why, like the apostle Paul before us, we so often do what we don't want to do and fail to do what we truly desire. As Paul famously wrote in Romans 7:15: "I do not understand what I do. For what I want to do I do not do, but what I hate I do."

When this inner conflict arises, our natural response is often shame, blame, and a sense of inadequacy. But is there a more redemptive way to respond, one that helps us unpack and understand what's really happening within us? And, just as importantly, are there ways we can recalibrate, find our centeredness in Christ's love, and discover a constructive way going forward by entrusting ourselves—imperfections and all—to the redemptive work of the Holy Spirit at work within us?

This book invites us into that deeper work. It helps us explore why we know we should love our neighbors as ourselves, yet so often fail to do so. Most of us don't neglect neighbor-love because we're indifferent or ignorant. For most folks, myself included, there are deeper issues at play beneath the surface when we fail to love our neighbors. Perhaps it's unprocessed trauma, social anxiety, a lack of practical tools, or the overwhelming sense that our neighbor's needs exceed our capacity.

As we sit with these tensions and try to discern how to respond, life doesn't pause. In the very moments we're seeking to show up, speak up, or stand with our neighbors, our child may come rushing in with a fresh wound; another mass shooting may strike too close to home; a fellow congregant may be deported, leaving behind a spouse and children with new needs; or a loved one might call with news of a diagnosis or relapse. Within our best intentions, moments of authentic discernment can turn into paralysis—and ultimately into inaction. To the outside world, which is quick to judge, cancel, and dismiss, we may appear apathetic. But that's not actually the case.

Even when we know that the assumptions others make about us are untrue, we still feel the sting of being misunderstood, judged, and mischaracterized. More importantly, beyond public perception, how do we love ourselves in those moments when we fall short of our own standards? How do we remember who God says we are, even when our emotions, or the world, tell us otherwise? And how do we learn from those moments, ensuring that paralysis doesn't become a pattern, and that a moment of missional paralysis does not devolve into a lukewarm witness?

Most discipleship resources don't help us think through these deeply human, deeply spiritual scenarios. They rarely offer tangible tools to engage in the inner work that can free us to participate fully in the redemptive work God is already doing. But we must remember what 2 Corinthians 5:19 tells us: "God was reconciling the world to himself in Christ, not counting people's sins against them. And he has committed to us the message of reconciliation." The gospel is not just an invitation to personal transformation; it is a divine calling to join God's reconciling work in the world—as the hands and feet of Christ.

This redemptive work includes both the restoration of broken people and the reformation of broken systems, structures, and laws. Through the Holy Spirit, who brings life from death, we are empowered to partner with God in setting things right in the midst of a broken world.

We are living in a watershed moment, and we need believers who understand what Dr. King called "the fierce urgency of now." He said, "We are now faced with the fact that tomorrow is today. We are confronted with the fierce urgency of now. In this unfolding conundrum of life and history, there is such a thing as being too late. This is no time for apathy or complacency. This is a time for vigorous and positive action." You are reading this book at a moment in time that strongly parallels the times when King spoke these words.

In the midst of being earthen vessels full of anxiety, inadequacies, insecurities, and trauma, 2 Corinthians 4:7 reminds us, "But we have this treasure in clay jars, so that it may be made clear that this extraordinary power belongs to God and does not come from us." We need Christian resources that holistically equip us to follow Jesus, and you will be blessed by the succeeding pages, which do exactly that.

Dominique DuBois Gilliard

Director of Racial Righteousness and Reconciliation,
Evangelical Covenant Church

Author of *Subversive Witness: Scripture's Call to Leverage Privilege* and *Rethinking Incarceration: Advocating for Justice That Restores*

INTRODUCTION

Among Christians, there is very little disagreement that we are called to love our neighbor. In divisive and highly polarized political climates, however, the questions "Who is my neighbor?" and "What counts as loving them?" are considerably more contentious. Perhaps one of the reasons Christians often struggle to come to a shared vision on how to best love our neighbor is that Jesus often told stories rife with both literal and figurative meanings intended to disrupt, complicate, and foster growth among those who were listening. Unfortunately, many of us resist this challenge.

In this book, we will explore the questions "Why do I struggle to love my neighbor?" and "How can I love better?" Studies in psychology and theology have harmonious insights that can help us unpack these questions. As a practical theologian (Katie) and psychological scientist (Brittany), we came to this shared conclusion through our friendship. Casual conversations about the courses we were teaching, the research we were conducting, and the experiences we were having led to many aha moments when we could see the ways that our fields were not in conflict, but rather pointing to similar conclusions about what it means to love others well and how challenging it can be to do so.

We began working together when Seattle Pacific University hosted a homeless encampment for a few months. Both of us were interested in how our students could love these unhoused neighbors. Our early conversations turned into a research project, some of which we will share in chapter 5, and eventually this book. This book is a compilation of our conversations and revelations about how the study of psychology and theology can mutually inform one another. For the sake of clarity and consistency, we write with a unified voice unless we're describing distinct personal experiences. But you'll know that we have complementary areas of expertise (Katie, theology, and Brittany, psychology) that have shaped the interdisciplinary insights we offer in this book.

The psychological research we will share with you will help you to develop a deeper understanding of how your own thoughts, emotions, and environment can sneakily undermine your goal to live and love faithfully. Through this work, we hope to offer you new tools and strategies that can be readily implemented into your life to reduce the struggle we all experience when trying to emulate Jesus's life and love.

You might be coming into this book thinking that research just confirms what we already know, or you might be asking yourself what science could possibly contribute to your faith life. Focusing on what science and theology do and do not do might be helpful. Theology answers questions related to who and why—it can tell us about who God is, who we are, and why we are called to behave in a particular way (for example, why should we love our neighbor). For Christians, theology helps us to discern moral imperatives. Science does not dabble in the "shoulds" and "should nots"; rather, it focuses on questions related to what and how. These questions are valuable as we consider *what* factors shape our willingness to engage with our neighbors and *how* we can do so in a way that is received as loving.

As Christians, we have a common call to love. We are told in countless passages to love one another as Jesus loved us. And yet, we know how difficult this is in reality. We all have those people in our life that feel hard to love and, if we are honest, ones we do not really want to love or feel it is our job to love. As Paul writes in Romans 7:15, we want to do good, but we often fail to do so—and sometimes we even do the very thing we do not want to do. One of the benefits of having psychological insights (in addition to praying that the Spirit would guide us and give us strength) is that you do not have to rely on your willpower alone in any given moment to act how you want to act. There are actually small changes you can make to your life and the ways that you interact with people that will help you love them better. As you read these chapters, we pray that you will be compelled to curate your life in a way that maximizes the frequency and quality of your engagement with others, not because we guilt you into it, but because you are more aware of common roadblocks that get in the way. In essence, we hope to make it easier for you to do what you already want to do, to love better.

Each chapter begins with "Learning from Psychology," a section that details key psychological studies or findings that will help you grow in self-awareness. These psychological insights promote actions that help others (called *prosocial behaviors* by psychologists) and quality interactions between people (called *interpersonal interactions* by psychologists). From a theological perspective, these studies champion ways to love your neighbor and pinpoint common factors that get in the way. Key psychological concepts appear in *italics*. If you would like to read the original studies, you can find the citations in the glossary.

These research insights are followed by a section titled "Thinking Theologically" which highlights biblical passages that exemplify the insights from psychological research or have parallel themes. These passages are read and interpreted through a theological lens, with relevant terms and concepts also appearing in *italics* for those wishing to do a deeper dive into their origin.

The final section, "Living Faithfully," offers ways to put your faith into action by suggesting opportunities to change your environment, embrace self-reflection, or engage a neighbor in a new way that's emboldened by psychological insight. Some of these strategies will be simple and easy to implement in your everyday life. Others might challenge the way you live on a deeper level, inviting you to restructure your life in ways that you may find disruptive or uncomfortable. If you take on these challenges, we believe they will help draw you closer to God and to others.

A bit more about us. We are scholars, colleagues, Christians, mothers, and friends. Like you, we are also working on loving better. All the things we write about are really hard to live out. We are each on a journey of becoming more like Christ that is shaped by where we started, the families and towns we were raised in, the identities and roles that we inhabit, the personal and educational experiences we have had, and the people who have loved us along our own paths. We share what follows as an invitation to grow in your faith, based not only on good theology but also the best insights that the field of psychology has to offer Christians regarding the call to love one another.

To get started, we have put together a short quiz to test your knowledge about the psychology of helping behaviors and social connections. Be bold, mark your answers in pen if you want, and let us know how you did. You can connect with us on our Substack https://lovingbetter.substack.com. We would love to hear from you!

---

1. True / False: Empathy is more like a fixed trait (something that you are born with) than a skill that can be developed.

2. True / False: If there are a lot of people present at an emergency, there is a greater likelihood that someone will intervene and do so quickly.

3. True / False: Serving meals at a soup kitchen is one of the best ways to reduce negative beliefs about individuals experiencing homelessness.

4. Who do you think would be *least* likely to help a stranger who is hurt? Someone who is in a ______.

    a. good mood
    b. hurry
    c. nerve-racking situation
    d. new environment

5. What factor is most important to explain whether relationships will form?

    a. attractiveness
    b. proximity
    c. similarity
    d. personality

6. When it comes to helping behaviors, Christians . . .

    a. are more likely than non-Christians to help others, in general
    b. are more likely than non-Christians to help others who are also Christians
    c. are less likely than non-Christians to help others, in general
    d. are less likely than non-Christians to help others who are also Christians

7. In an apartment building, who is especially likely to have friends on a floor other than their own?

    a. people high in extroversion
    b. people high in loneliness
    c. people who live near the stairs
    d. people who live in the smallest apartments

8. Which emotion is the most damaging in relationships / predictive of divorce?

    a. criticism
    b. contempt
    c. defensiveness
    d. stonewalling

9. Who is most likely to help someone in need?

    a. someone who grew up in a small town
    b. someone who grew up in a big city
    c. someone who is visiting a small town
    d. someone who is visiting a big city

10. Psychological research has demonstrated that electronic devices, like cell phones, only decrease the quality of interpersonal connections when they are used three or more times during an interaction. Do you find this surprising? Why or why not?

You will find the answers to these quiz questions throughout the book as you learn about the corresponding psychological studies. (The quiz answers are provided in endnotes.) As for the last question, if you are like most of our students, you do not find it surprising that cell phones decrease the quality of interpersonal connections if they are used three or more times. You likely even generated some compelling reasons as to why. The big reveal? That is not what research has shown. It is a fake conclusion. There is not a "magic number" of cell phone uses that harm an interaction. Cell phones harm interactions even if they are never used at all.

We will tell you even more about this research and the ways devices harm relationships in chapter 3. For now, any response about why this was not surprising helps demonstrate a principle referred to as *hindsight bias*, the tendency for something to feel obvious after the answer is known. Hindsight bias is something all people experience, and it can undermine the way you engage new information. As you read this book, you might identify places where roadblocks to loving your neighbor seem obvious, and other places where you may have been less aware of the factors that are getting in your way. Either way, we hope that orienting your attention to these common barriers will help you to feel more equipped to live into Christ's call to love your neighbor. You could read this book alone or with a group. However you engage, it is our prayer that by the end you will have grown in love for your neighbor, for God, and for yourself.

part one

WHEN CIRCUMSTANCES GET IN THE WAY OF LOVING YOUR NEIGHBOR

one

NOTICING YOUR NEIGHBOR

"And who is my neighbor?"

—Luke 10:29

LEARNING FROM PSYCHOLOGY

What if we told you we could predict which of your neighbors you are friends with, without knowing anything about you, or your neighbors for that matter? This might seem unlikely, but decades of social psychological research devoted to determining when friendships and romantic relationships will form have zeroed in on a few key principles that predict, on average, social connections. The number one predictor? It is not how similar you are, the number of shared interests you have, or anything related to personality. It's proximity.[1] The person that is physically located closest to you is the person you are most likely to befriend. Chances are you are better friends, or at least more well acquainted, with your neighbors that live immediately next door to you than your neighbors two or three houses down. This is not because you happen to have the most in common with your neighbors immediately next door but because they happen to live closest to you.

At face value, it makes sense—if two people are never in the same place at the same time, how would they ever connect or get to know one another. What is more surprising is how drastically an increase in distance can reduce your likelihood of connection. Studies that explore whether *proximity* predicts how much people like one another often track the formation of friendships within living spaces like apartment complexes. What these observations reveal is that people are most likely to be friends with someone who lives immediately next door or across the hall from them. The likelihood of friendship declines with each door that is more distant from your own. The odds of considering an immediately adjacent neighbor a friend? 41 percent. One door removed? 22 percent. Two doors down? 10 percent.

With each door we cut nearly in half the likelihood that we will consider those in our physical space our friends. Having students map out their college dorm rooms and their closest friends tends to reveal a similar trend in an eerie and somewhat fatalistic way. What about you? If you went to (or are currently attending) college, draw a map of your freshman college dorm and your friends that year. Or draw a map of your current neighborhood and friends. In your life, have your friendships formed with those who lived the closest to you?

If you would not consider any of your neighbors friends, we can lower the stakes: How about acquaintances, folks you can at least name and perhaps even know a bit about? Here, on the opposite page, is one of ours.

It is a bit unnerving to think that if you had simply roomed with someone else or been assigned to a corner room a bit further down the hall, you might not have established some of the lifelong relationships that are often formed in college. The same rings true for which of your neighbors is most likely to be joining you for dinner or the colleagues with whom you grab drinks after work.

One caveat to the idea that proximity promotes friendship is that physical closeness does not always translate to ease of con-

Don't know at all.
Know general information about. They are fellow Wyoming folks and host football viewing parties in their garage-turned-outside-living room.
Have only ever spoken via text after they backed into my car, seem really nice though!
Know relatively well. Firefighter and avid runners. Three boys and very generous with old toys and clothes. Sole reason my kids have a power wheels jeep.
Recently had a baby, make great banana bread, on a general acquaintance basis.
Don't know at all.
Newest neighbors. Names only. Calls me Britney Spears, in my head I call him Carlos Santana.
Know relatively well. A really sweet family with two kids. They help us get our oldest to school when our baby is sick, have a dog named Ozzie, and take epic family photos!
OUR HOUSE
Know general information about, and occasionally connect to have our puppies play together.
Don't know at all.
Don't know at all.
Don't know at all.
Know his name. Peed in our backyard once. We now have a fence.
British expat and American dog lover. Make delicious split pea soup and enjoy eating salmon for special holiday meals.

nection. We both live in the heart of Seattle where space is a luxury most people do not have, and many park their cars on the street. As a result, hardly a day goes by when we do not interact with at least one of our immediate neighbors. Most of these encounters tend to happen as we are similarly loading up droves of tiny humans to get to work and school.

If you happen to live in a suburban area with a garage you park your car in, on a ranch in Wyoming with acres of land around you, or somewhere similarly removed from other folks, you may not ever accidentally bump into your neighbors in a way that facilitates organic interactions. If your living situation fits one of these models more closely, then another psychological principle—the *propinquity effect*—might help to explain why your neighbors are less likely to be your friends. It can also help to explain the spontaneous friendships you do develop.

If you have ever seen a sitcom from the '90s featuring salacious gossip sessions at a water cooler, you are already familiar with the basic principles of the propinquity effect. In essence, places where people gather or cross paths frequently spontaneously promote friendships. Psychological studies on spontaneous friendships have shown, surprisingly, that people who have formed office friendships with individuals that do not sit immediately next to them (or have an office right next door) often had their desks or offices near high-traffic areas such as elevators, stairs, or mailboxes.[2] Working next to these public watering holes sparks spontaneous friendships in the same way as bumping into your neighbor every day while unloading groceries or kids. Such opportunities for engagement are critical, not only because they facilitate friendships but also because they can challenge you to think about how you let the physical spaces you inhabit dictate whom you do (and do not) see as a neighbor.

Underneath both proximity and propinquity is one other important psychological factor that predicts liking: *familiarity*. The more familiar we are with people, the more likely we are to like them. This familiarity does not have to be overt—it can actually happen on a very subtle and even nonconscious level through repeated exposure to the same person (seeing them over and over again), even if we don't always realize that they are there. Psychologists call the tendency to like something more the more you are exposed to it the *mere exposure effect*.

In one study that illustrates this effect, researchers had a fake student sit in on either one, a few, or several classes throughout the quarter. At the end of the quarter, real students in the classes were asked to rate how much they liked the fake student. The real students reported liking the fake student more the more classes they attended together, not necessarily because they directly interacted with that student more, but simply because the student was more familiar to them. What is familiar is often considered good, and what is unfamiliar is often considered less good. Being aware of this can help us to be intentional about why we may be more inclined to think of some people as neighbors (in the biblical sense) than others. It can also help us to ask honest questions about why we may feel more inclined to help some people than others.

Psych Summary: How you inhabit physical space matters. Proximity creates opportunities to connect with and love others, or it can cut you off from opportunities to witness the needs of others. The closer you can be to others physically, the more opportunities you have to get to know them and the more opportunities you have to love them. When your environment creates natural distance, you can seek out shared or common public spaces, putting yourself in the paths of others so that you can share God's love with all those you encounter.

THINKING THEOLOGICALLY

> Just then a lawyer stood up to test Jesus. "Teacher," he said, "What must I do to inherit eternal life?" He said to him, "What is written in the law? What do you read there?" He

> answered, "You shall love the Lord your God with all your heart, and with all your soul, and with all your strength, and with all your mind; and your neighbor as yourself." And he said to him, "You have given the right answer; do this, and you will live."
>
> But wanting to justify himself, he asked Jesus, "And who is my neighbor?"
>
> —Luke 10:25–29

If you are familiar with the biblical passage above, you know that the story does not end there. After offering his summary of the law, the lawyer challenges Jesus with a seemingly cheeky question, "And who is my neighbor?"[3] While we cannot be sure what the intention of the lawyer was at that moment, one interpretation is that they want permission from God to love certain people and not others, likely those who were the most like them and had similar religious beliefs. Perhaps sensing this desire, Jesus responds with the story of the good Samaritan. In this parable, Jesus describes three people who encounter a man who was robbed and left injured by robbers. In the parable, only the third, a Samaritan, stops to help. Jesus then asks, "Which of these three, do you think, was a neighbor to the man who fell into the hands of the robbers?" (Luke 10:36).

Your Neighbor Is Not Just Next Door

A common literal interpretation of "neighbor" requires that we think about those who are adjacent in our physical residence, like who lives next door or has an office near ours. On the surface, then, the parable is already strange because the Samaritan and the Jewish man were definitely not neighbors. They did not live next door to one another. They were from wildly different places. It might be tempting to stop there and say that Jesus is simply expanding the definition of *neighbor* to include more than just those folks who live immediately next door or in your neighborhood, widening the definition to include those whose proximity promotes a neighborly connection. Even stopping here, many of us have significant room for growth. Friendships with those immediately next door in the apartment study were far from 100 percent. In the book *The Art of Neighboring*, the authors point out that many of us struggle to name those who live in our neighborhood (this may have been true in your own map).[4] Of course, you cannot love people you do not know and you *should* work to cultivate connections with the folks two and even three doors down. But what else is there to learn from this parable aside from, be neighborly to those both in and beyond your physical neighborhood?

Your Neighbor Is Not Just Those Who Are Similar to You

Pushing deeper, countless sermons have been preached on the metaphors present in Jesus's response to the lawyer and how they disrupt our desire to love those who are familiar to or like us in some way. And that is true. The Samaritan and the Jewish man did not know or recognize one another. They seem to have very little, if anything at all, in common. By considering the historical context, we are able to appreciate additional complexity. These two individuals came from lands that were politically, religiously, and ethnically divided. Describing the origin of the conflict in this story, reconciliation studies professor Brenda Salter McNeil emphasizes that their "differences" went beyond living in different locations or believing different things to a cultural hostility that drove intentional separation.[5] Jesus uses this story to emphasize that neighbors are not just those who live in close proximity to you or those to whom you are socially, politically, religiously, or otherwise similar. Neighbors are also those who belong to groups society has set you up to dislike or actively avoid.

Your Neighbor Is Wherever You Are

The encounter becomes increasingly perplexing when considering the proximity and propinquity effects. The Samaritan and the Jewish man should have never ended up in the same place at the same time. The Jewish man was likely going out of his way to avoid passing directly through Samaria, as most Jews did, and yet, it was a Samaritan who came to his rescue. What this seems to imply, then, is that the people whom we come across and randomly bump into, even those who don't like us and actively avoid us, are our neighbors. The next obvious question, then, is, Where am I? Am I putting myself in spaces to spontaneously engage with others? What about others who don't like me? In the world of theology, this has been called *enacted space*. This concept recognizes that the environments in which we live, the places we frequent, the paths we travel, and how we travel them, all promote or prohibit connection with others and thus our opportunity to participate in the work God is already doing around us. This was certainly the case for the good Samaritan, who could have never been "a neighbor" to the Jewish man if it were not for the fact that they were traveling along the same road at the same time.

According to this parable, neighbors are not just those who live around us, and not just those who are different from us, but anyone and everyone with whom our paths cross. Studies on proximity help us to see how narrow our scope of *neighbor* has become, limited to (maybe) those who are immediately next door. The propinquity effect emphasizes how incredibly important it is to locate ourselves in spaces that give us the opportunity to be neighborly. Those who are near me at any given point in time—they are my neighbors. Those whose paths I cross virtually online—they are my neighbors. Those whom I drive past on my way to work—they are my neighbors. Those whom I encounter when traveling abroad—they are my neighbors. Those whom I actively try to avoid and still bump into running errands—they are my neighbors. Jesus challenged a traditional definition of *neighbor*, teaching us that our neighbors are wherever we find ourselves at any given point in time. While the goal here is not to dissuade you from loving others that are located at a distance, we believe there is something to be said for the type of love that can be shared and sustained through an embodied encounter. In part, this is true because such encounters, in all their messiness, have the opportunity to transform us as well.

Think about it for yourself—do you have a habit of moving through your day in such a way that you never really encounter or engage with anyone unexpectedly? If the design of many modern neighborhoods (think long driveways and big garages) and increasingly individualistic routines (think frequenting a drive-through coffee shop rather than walking in or wearing headphones while grocery shopping) isolate us from everyone other than those we intentionally seek to spend time with, then we really are limiting our own neighborly impact. More pointedly, we are opting out of the call to love others beyond those who already love us in return. The Gospel of Luke points out that even the pagans love those who love them back. Christians are called to love better, to love broader (Luke 6:32–36).

LIVING FAITHFULLY

If you find yourself getting a bit defensive or scrambling to think of ways you intentionally love others whom you do not know well, who do not love you back, or who are dissimilar to you, that is great! What that defensiveness tells us is that you genuinely value and have already taken to heart the call to love those who don't—or can't—love you in return just like the good Samaritan did. In these reactions, you may be coming up with examples of how you volunteer or donate your time, and we will unpack those later, but for now, let us think about how you can live more faithfully by reframing the way you think about the places you regularly go and consider how you can be more intentional about putting yourself in spaces to have unexpected encounters.

So, here is your next challenge. Let's put together a new map—a daily routine map. On a typical day, where do you go, and who are the folks you encounter when you are there? How many of them do you know? How many of them would you consider friends? Could you speak into what they are struggling with? What is happening in their lives? How have you offered help to the people you bump into throughout your daily routine? Are there people you see regularly but have never spoken to?

Here is Katie's daily routine map:

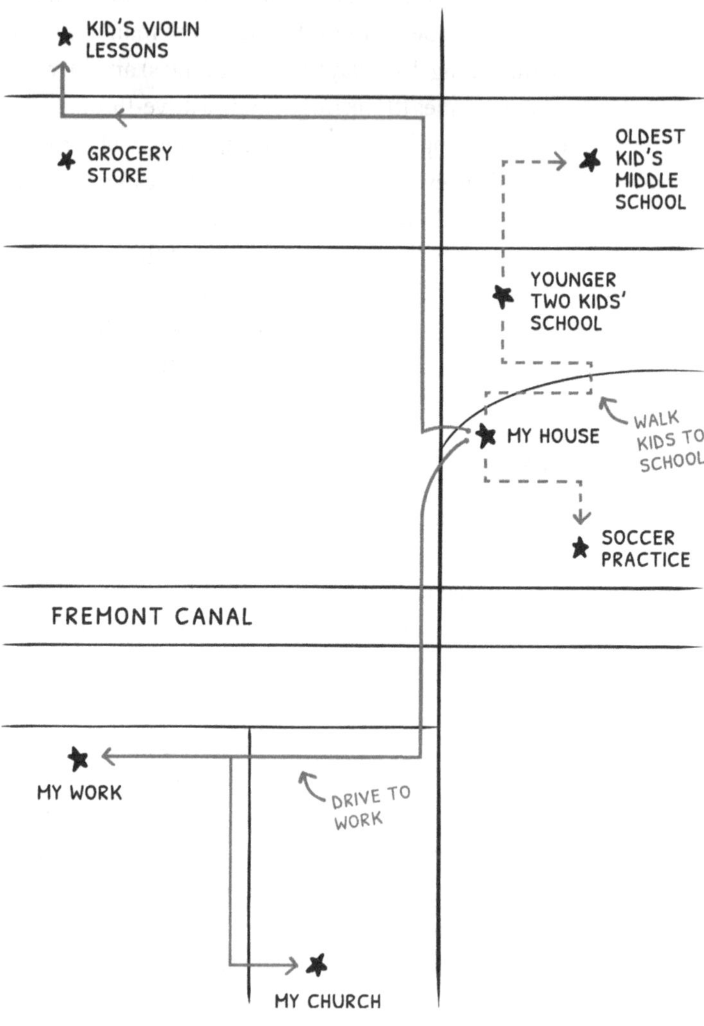

> My daily routine involves walking my 3 boys to school where I easily see 200 other parents, elementary kids, middle schoolers, crossing guards, bus drivers, and teachers before and after school every day. I am good friends with 8 to 10 of them and I talk with them almost daily. I sometimes bike to work, where I have a lot of interactions with other bike commuters, pedestrians, and people who are unhoused in Seattle. On rainy days I drive, which eliminates all of these interactions. Once I get to work, I see 30 to 60 students in class at least three days a week and 15–40 colleagues in various meetings. My weekly routine also involves taking my kids to youth group, music lessons, and soccer practice. I also go grocery shopping and to church at least once a week. Reflecting on this map, it's clear that I interact with far more people when I walk than when I drive. I also interact with more people when I go to campus to work rather than working from home.

What does your daily routine map look like? Draw it out in a notebook or on a piece of scrap paper to see where you are most likely to encounter other people.

You have now drawn two maps, a map of your neighborhood and a daily routine map to help you locate the people most likely to be your neighbors in multiple senses of the word—those who are physically proximate to you and those whose paths you cross. Now, take a moment to prayerfully reflect on your maps. Invite God to show you the places where you clearly and comfortably acknowledge someone as your neighbor as well as the places that feel less comfortable. As you pray, make a list of the names of people whose paths you cross daily. You might even write their names on the map. You might also include in the list descriptions of people that you pass each day. What shifts for you as you expand your definition of neighbor to include all of these people?

Another option to live out new ways of noticing neighbors is to switch up your routine. Instead of driving to work, you could take the bus. Or rather than eating alone in your office or kitchen, what if you sat out on a park bench or in a shared space in your building?

Resisting the urge to avoid someone, perhaps because of differing political views, what if you simply made it a routine to say, "Good morning, how was your weekend?" when you see them.

As you begin your day tomorrow, pray that the Spirit will guide you in noticing those around you and seeing them with new eyes, as a neighbor whose needs to which you are called to attend, and whose presence has the potential to transform you . . . if you are open to it. In the natural pauses of your day—sitting at a traffic light, waiting for an elevator, standing in line at the grocery store, waiting to pick up your kids—begin to notice who is present with you. As you notice your neighbors in new ways, you might imagine new ways to love them. Loving better is about offering love to our neighbors in the places we already inhabit.

two

HURRYING LESS

Look, the tears of the oppressed—with no one to comfort them!

—Ecclesiastes 4:1

LEARNING FROM PSYCHOLOGY

When we consider the call to love our neighbor, one of the first questions we might ask is, What circumstances determine whether we will stop to help someone in need? In the previous chapter, we suggested that a primary hurdle is an overly narrow definition of "neighbor." A more expansive definition of "neighbor" (not just the people who live next door) is critical to emulating the life and love of Jesus. But accepting an "everyone I encounter everywhere, even if they don't like me, is my neighbor" mentality does not guarantee we will treat those people in a neighborly way. There are plenty of other circumstances that still thwart our best intentions to love those around us better. In this chapter, we will talk about one of the most insidious in Western cultures: a perceived lack of time.

The field of psychology has much to say about who will help and when. One famous study from the 1970s is called the Good Samaritan study. Researchers placed seminarians in a helping dilemma that mirrored the good Samaritan parable found in

Luke 10. A scene was staged in an alleyway between buildings on a college campus where a man was slumped over, moaned, and coughed twice as seminarians walked through the four-foot-wide space. Who would stop to help the man? Before the encounter the seminarians took a survey regarding the way they thought of their religious identity. Were they more of a Levite, concerned with what they gain from faith, or were they more of a Samaritan, thinking about faith as a quest? They were then told to go through the alley to the next building to give a talk—with varying levels of urgency. Some were told, "You have plenty of time." Others were told, "The meeting is about to start," and a third group was told, "Hurry, you are late!" Upon their arrival, they gave a talk they had prepared either on seminary job prospects or the parable of the good Samaritan. Researchers found that even though all the seminarians took a route that required them to pass by the man in need of help, only 40 percent stopped to offer some kind of assistance. So who were the 40 percent?

You might expect that the so-called "quest-ers," those that seemed to hold beliefs more similar to those of the Samaritan hero of the parable, would be more likely to help than those who held more self-focused beliefs (the Levitical "gain-ers"). But the researchers found no such relationship. Personal beliefs did not predict who helped—at all. Well, then, perhaps it wasn't what the seminarians *believed* as much as what they were thinking about at any given point in time that would influence their likelihood to help? In other words, maybe those whose faith was top of mind, due to preparing to talk about the good Samaritan parable, would be more likely to help. But again, that was not the case. The only factor that the researchers were able to identify as a significant predictor of who helped was time. Of those who were in the "high hurry" condition, only 10 percent stopped to help.[1] Things looked a bit better in the "medium hurry" condition: nearly half of those folks stopped to help (45 percent). In the "low hurry" condition, 63 percent stopped to help. Even with lots of time on their hands, this is still far from the 100 percent we might hope for (or even expect) with a group of seminarians, half of whom are getting ready to give a talk about the importance of stopping to help.[2]

We may be tempted to judge these folks or to righteously assume that we are certain we would have stopped to help if we were in the study, but it might be more helpful to recognize the bigger picture. What this study communicates so clearly is that the situation matters . . . a lot. This study identified that simply running late can make you less neighborly. This may rightly evoke images of the White Rabbit in Disney's *Alice in Wonderland* scurrying by saying, "I'm late, I'm late. No time to say hello. Goodbye. I'm late, I'm late, I'm late." It may also bring to mind a personal experience, like a time when you were running so behind you impatiently cut off a conversation with an elderly neighbor, a hurting friend, or a curious child. Listen to these nudges. Sometimes the best thing we can do to be more neighborly is to create the conditions (ahem, leaving early) that cultivate care and connection.

Let's do a quick mental imagery exercise to think about how hurrying impacts your life. Close your eyes and imagine moving about your day. Start with how you wake up in the morning (to an alarm? to a crying baby? to the sound of birds chirping, cows mooing, or coffee grinding?) all the way through until you crawl into your bed for the night. Seriously. Try it. Set two minutes on your phone timer (we know your phone is right next to you). We will wait. . . .

All right, the initial awkwardness is over and you have gone through your day. So let's do it again. This time, instead of focusing on what you are doing, focus on how you feel. What parts of your day feel the most rushed or the most chaotic? What parts of your day feel the most relaxed? One way to determine this is to tune into what is happening in your body during this mental simulation. You might notice clenching your jaw or tightening your shoulders while imagining the morning circus that is trying to get yourself and your kids out the door for an appointment. You may feel your forehead relax and the frenetic speed of your thoughts slow when imagining the familiar walk through your local park. You may notice your heart begin to race or a pit in your stomach grow when thinking about a difficult conversation you need to have. Listen to what your body is telling you as you mentally navigate your day. Use the experience of tension versus relaxation, frantic versus manageable energy to help you identify the most chaotic and the calmest parts of your day. You can use this template to help you.

CHAOS AND CALM

I notice ______________________________ in my body when imagining ____________________ part of my day. This is a calm / chaotic (circle one) part of my day.

I notice ______________________________ in my body when imagining ____________________ part of my day. This is a calm / chaotic (circle one) part of my day.

I notice ______________________________ in my body when imagining ____________________ part of my day. This is a calm / chaotic (circle one) part of my day.

I notice ______________________________ in my body when imagining ____________________ part of my day. This is a calm / chaotic (circle one) part of my day.

Walking through this exercise can help to illuminate the times throughout your day when you are the most (calm) and least (chaotic) likely to love others well, not because you are a bad or uncaring person but simply because chaos is not conducive to noticing the needs of those around you. When you are calm, relaxed, and unhurried, you are able to be curious about and responsive to the needs of others. When you are feeling frantic and tense, you will be more inwardly focused. And this makes sense. In these moments of chaos, your body is sending you signals (e.g., physical pain, racing thoughts) that either demand attention or action. Remember, just like we learned from the Good Samaritan psychology study, feeling frantic or like you don't have enough time is likely to greatly reduce your support for others. This is true even if you believe it is important to help and you are actively thinking about the importance of helping. To be a good neighbor, then, might require not a change of heart or theology, but rather a change of schedule.

That having enough time is a better indicator of who will help than many of the other factors we might assume matter more (e.g., beliefs, current thoughts or mood) is just one example of the many useful insights that can be gleaned from social psychological research. Other work highlights additional factors that may be similarly underestimated or easy to overlook. Findings from this research can be distilled into steps, often referred to as the *stages of helping*, that predict when folks help. These are as follows:

1. Did I notice the event?
2. Did I interpret the event as an emergency?
3. Did I feel it was my responsibility to help?
4. Did I know how to help?
5. Did I think that the cost of helping would be relatively minimal?

According to this framework, if we answer no (whether consciously or not) to any one of these questions, it is unlikely that we will help. In the Good Samaritan study, most of those who failed to help likely did so because they did not complete even the first step—simply noticing the man in need of help.

Even when people did have enough time, however, still not everyone stopped to help. It is possible this is because those individuals were experiencing internal chaos. Very few folks love speaking in public, especially with little warning and preparation. Many (if not all) were probably feeling their hearts and minds racing as they made their way (even slowly) over to the location of their talk on campus. In other words, people may have failed to notice the pain of another for a variety of both internal (what is going on in our own heads) and external (we have to rush to get somewhere on time) reasons. Let us repeat: This does not mean people are, in general, bad or unhelpful, but it might mean that people are not great at setting themselves up to notice the needs of those around them. It could also mean that one or more of the other stages of helping was not met. We will begin to unpack those more in future chapters.

Psych Summary: Noble thoughts about helping others and beliefs about one's call to help are not enough to guarantee seminarians will help someone in need. Instead, something far more mundane appears to be a stronger indicator of who helps: time. In a hurry? Even the most agreeable and caring among us are less likely to stop and help someone in need. Have time to spare? Then most of us who value our call to care for the sick and the hurting would be considerably more likely to stop and help.

Can you imagine if Jesus only helped when he did not have somewhere else to be or something else to be doing? If we know that being in a hurry makes us less likely to love our neighbor, as we are so clearly called to do, then perhaps this research can be a nudge to help us reconsider whether our schedules are setting us up for success or failure to meet that call.

THINKING THEOLOGICALLY

> Again I saw all the oppressions that are practiced under the sun. Look, the tears of the oppressed—with no one to comfort them! On the side of their oppressors there was power—with

no one to comfort them. And I thought the dead, who have already died, more fortunate than the living, who are still alive; but better than both is the one who has not yet been, and has not seen the evil deeds that are done under the sun.

Then I saw that all toil and all skill in work come from one person's envy of another. This also is vanity and a chasing after wind.

Fools fold their hands
  and consume their own flesh.
Better is a handful with quiet
  than two handfuls with toil,
  and a chasing after wind.

Again, I saw vanity under the sun: the case of solitary individuals, without sons or brothers; yet there is no end to all their toil, and their eyes are never satisfied with riches. "For whom am I toiling," they ask, "and depriving myself of pleasure?" This also is vanity and an unhappy business.

—Ecclesiastes 4:1–8

On one level, the entire book of Ecclesiastes is about time and how we are to spend it. The author of Ecclesiastes is concerned with the questions, What is a good life, and How should we live it? We are admonished to enjoy the details of our lives, to seize the day by eating bread and drinking wine with a merry heart (Eccles. 7:9). But we are quickly reminded that the good die young and some who are evil seem to have their life prolonged by their evil deeds (Eccles. 7:15). Despite this randomness, the author of Ecclesiastes sees a pattern, marked in time (Eccles. 3). We are not to be driven to the extremes of despair or naive hope, but rather to see how time is marked by seasons that are, in some ways, predictable. When we can anticipate these, and hold onto the truth that God is present in all times, we are freed from the insatiable drive to do more, achieve more, gain more.

Freedom from the drive to constantly progress and accomplish more allows us to notice the people before us, to become witnesses and companions as they experience the ebb and flow of pain and joy in their lives. Freedom from hurry gives us the space to intentionally participate in the lives of others. Ecclesiastes gives us permission to slow down and to be the kind of person that we want to be—the kind of person who notices the pain of others, assumes responsibility, and offers real help in response. In the opening lines of Ecclesiastes 4, the author writes, "Look, the tears of the oppressed—with no one to comfort them!" (v. 1). This is followed by the critique of working too much and the competition that it breeds.

The author of Ecclesiastes is not so subtly suggesting that the oppressors are distracted by work and accumulating wealth that does not ultimately satisfy. The alternative is to seek something other than success, achievement, and accumulation. This is not to say that we should give up on work, but it does mean that we should resist the temptation to allow work to consume all our time and attention. Instead, perhaps, a meaningful life might be found in making space in our lives to notice, listen to, respond to, and comfort those crying out around us. Ironically, when we orient ourselves toward others it can feel like we receive even more than we have given. You have probably had an experience when you felt like you received more than you gave when you connected with those who were suffering. This phenomenon has been referred to as the *paradox of generosity*.

The author of Ecclesiastes is critical of those of us who are too busy to be present, too busy to notice. Not only do we fail to help them, but we fail to receive the gifts they offer us. This section begins with the imperative to "Look!" Notice! See the oppressed! The author goes on to say, Don't just see them; see how they are unnoticed, lacking attention because of a world filled with people who are distracted. The wealth accumulated by endless work or toil cannot go with you after you die. The wealth that your work can accumulate does not ultimately satisfy. And our work or busy calendars can distract us from having a life slow enough to experience the gift of a simple meal with those we love and perhaps, even more profoundly, our work distracts us from seeing the tears of the oppressed.

One way to think about the Good Samaritan study and its impact on our faith is in regard to the pace of our life and how that affects our ability to notice and offer our attention to those whom God has placed in our lives. French philosopher and theologian Simone Weil wrote about our attention as one of the greatest gifts we can give to another person. Here is one of her incredible quotes about the power of love when we slow our pace enough to notice and listen to people.

> The capacity to give one's attention to a sufferer is a very rare and difficult thing; it is almost a miracle; it is a miracle. . . . The love of our neighbor in all its fullness simply means being able to say, "What are you going through?"[3]

Are we living slowly enough to take the time to ask those whose paths we cross, "What are you going through?" and then sit with them, listening, for as long as it takes to hear their response? According to Weil, this is God's love working through us. When we love our neighbor, we are loving God.

LIVING FAITHFULLY

Based on these insights from Scripture and psychology, we want to invite you to prayerfully reorient yourself to your schedule, your time, and your attention. Researchers have found people always assume they will be able to do more in the future than they can actually do, because they underestimate how long things will take. This is called the *planning fallacy*. Disappointingly, simply knowing about the fallacy does not help people to avoid it. We remain woefully optimistic that we will be able to accomplish more in less time in the future.

The cost of this fallacy is high. Our schedules are packed to the brim with no room to just be, let alone notice the needs of those around us. A more reliable approach to counter the planning fallacy is to intentionally overestimate how long things will take you. For example, if you believe that it will only take you fifteen minutes to run to the grocery store, you can set aside thirty minutes in your schedule for the task. The more complex the task, the more you should overestimate. Rather than relying on your intuition regarding time, we invite you to give attention, through the following activities, to your own schedule and the ways you experience time.

Take out your calendar or revisit your daily routine map from chapter 1 and prayerfully ask God to reveal things to you. Where are spaces you might be called to give your full attention and presence? When we led this exercise with college students, we began to rethink our own schedules and see the school drop-off and pick-up parts of our daily routine as times to listen to and connect with other parents who were exhausted, managing a new ADHD diagnosis, struggling with infertility, or navigating how to care for aging parents.

Turn your attention to your daily schedule—not just the places you go, but how busy your days are. A quick way to assess this (if you are not a big calendar person) is to consider the following: When was the last time someone asked you how you were doing and you said something to the effect of "busy, but good"? For many of us this is a pretty standard response. It may be your season of life. You might have a three-year-old and a one-year-old at home and feel like you are juggling what feels like all of the things with none of the sleep. You might be caring for sick family members, working multiple jobs to make ends meet, or in the middle of a big project that feels all consuming. Even in these busy seasons, it is important to remember that we are never helpless. There are always ways to adjust the frenetic pace of our internal and external worlds. We may need to say no to good things and have faith that other good things will come. We may need to ask for help even when we don't want to or it is difficult. We may need to turn off our cell phones (more on that later!). We may need to interrogate whether we have bought into the notion that "time is money" and busyness is a badge of honor.

While anyone can practice embodying time differently, it is worth acknowledging how culture can influence the way that we think (and talk) about time.[4] Some fascinating psychology studies have demonstrated that many people in Western cultures use metaphors like "looking forward" to the future and "looking back" on the past. But these metaphors are not universal. The Aymara people in the Andes, for example, speak about the future being behind them (because it is what is unseen or unknown) and the past being in front of them because it is what is seen and known! It isn't just metaphors that vary across culture, so does the value we place on the past, present, and future.[5] If you find yourself always rushing to the next thing, this may serve as an indicator that you are currently embedded in or have been deeply shaped by a "future-focused" culture that is always looking for the next thing.

If you have ever had the opportunity to travel abroad or to get to know someone from a different country, you may have noticed subtle (or not so subtle) ways in which you approach time differently. How long is too long for a shared meal together? When should a server deliver a check? How important is it to be on time for an appointment? How quickly do you walk when completing (hello, running) errands? One of our colleagues, Cara Wall-Scheffler, and her undergraduate student Leah Bouterse published a research study on walking speeds of people in Uganda and the United States.[6] Interestingly, their research demonstrated that when walking solo, Ugandans walked faster than Americans. However, when they were walking with other people (including their children), Americans walked faster and Ugandans walked slower.

That the Americans were quick to speed up in groups resonates with our personal experiences that time by yourself is when you slow down, but when others are involved, we find ourselves moving at a quicker, less leisurely pace. We both have several friends from different countries who counter the "stay busy" narrative in powerful ways. They tend to both arrive at and leave from birthday parties or other gatherings much later than expected. They also have a comfortable patience and presence about them that never suggests you are wasting their "precious" time or they are eager to move on to the next part of their day. These differences can feel disorienting at times or even inconvenient. Approaching the situation with what psychologists call *cultural humility* can help us remember that different things are considered correct or polite in different places and that there is something to be learned and celebrated in every culture. God did create us all, after all.

Recognizing the potential to learn from different cultural approaches to time, you can reframe (unexpectedly) extended visits as opportunities to love your neighbors well. The slower pace during moments when there are fewer people around can provide unique opportunities for connection. Inevitably conversations happen that wouldn't have otherwise, and there are moments of undivided attention that ensure everyone feels more seen, heard, and loved. If we "hurry up" and "hurry out," or signal to others that they need to, we may miss opportunities to love the way that Jesus loved.

In John 11 we see a striking example of Jesus moving slowly, taking his time, and prioritizing what was right in front of him rather than the next thing. When Mary and Martha sent word to Jesus that Lazarus was sick, we are told that Jesus "stayed two days longer in the place where he was" (John 11:6). This feels like a critical emergency, when fast moves and abrupt departures are not only warranted but downright necessary, especially considering commute times back then. Being Jesus, he likely had many good reasons for waiting to go to Judea to see Lazarus, and yet we are not told what Jesus did during those two days or why he needed to stay. It is just clear that he waited.

One possible interpretation of why Jesus waited is that he did not care about Mary and Martha and Lazarus. It certainly seems to have felt this way to Mary and Martha. An alternative interpretation is that Jesus did care about them (of course he did!), but that he also cared about the people right in front of him, where he was currently located. Jesus's decision to wait and not rush off signaled that the people he was currently with mattered to him too. The people right in front of us are, after all, the neighbors we are being called to love. Being generous with your time and not constantly rushing off to the next thing (no matter how important it might seem) is one way that we can emulate the countercultural love of Jesus.

When was the last time you intentionally showed up for something early or left late for no reason other than to give yourself extra time to be present and connect with whoever happens to be around? Our guess is that your schedule is so jam-packed this doesn't even feel like an option for you. So, here are a few suggestions. Based on where you are in your own life, pick one or two to try out this week.

---

1. Revisit the chaos and calm mental imagery exercise that you completed and consider the following:

   a. What is one small step you could take to reduce a bit of the chaos or introduce a bit of calm to that part of your day? Could you pack your bags the night before, or set your alarm a few minutes early? Could you have your kids sleep in what they want to wear to school the next day? Maybe all you can do is light a candle in the morning to remind yourself of God's presence as you prepare for the day. It might not change how much you need to accomplish, but changing the ambiance could bring a sense of calm or simply a visible reminder that God is with you in the chaos.

b. For the parts of your day that feel calmer, how can you embrace those moments more fully? Rather than checking emails or texts at every stoplight, what if you just drove home in silence, using your commute to appreciate your neighborhood, the seasonal changes, or perhaps even to think about the kinds of interactions you want to have with your family when you get home.

2. Look at your schedule and prayerfully consider what to take off your list or how to create space between events. Are there things that keep your schedule full but are not necessary? Are you packing your calendar to a point where there is no time to breathe?

   a. Create Blackout Dates. Spend some time looking at your calendar as a whole and create "blackout dates" during extra busy times when you will not plan additional activities. It may be helpful to intentionally plan zero activities after school or on the weekend for the first two weeks of a new school year. This might allow you and your family to reacclimate to the pace. This intentional effort to do nothing can result in a calmer start to the year, and help establish strong routines that will make the rest of the year easier. Perhaps you aren't in school or don't have kids who are, but the last week of every month at work tends to be extra busy for you. Could you treat that week every month (or at least a few days of it) as a "blackout" week when you do not schedule extra activities?

   b. Create Time Buffers. What parts of your day feel the most rushed? Rather than back-to-back meetings, can you schedule fifteen-minute breaks in between that will help you be fully present for each person you interact with? When counselors and doctors do this with their patients, it is noticeable. Some are staring at the clock and rushing you out what feels like a revolving door. Others have created enough of a buffer that the appointments can wrap up more organically.

3. Reconsider how you approach time:

    a. Consider showing up intentionally early for something, just to be present and see what God has in store.

    b. If you find yourself in a new environment (any travelers out there?!) or interacting with someone who has a different approach to time, how can you embrace the discomfort with curiosity? If things aren't moving at a pace (or in a way) that feels typical for you and you find yourself getting frustrated, can you shift your mindset away from the future? Instead of "What comes next," "God, how can I love the people right in front of me at this moment?" Instead of "Can't we move things along here," how about you take the time to reflect on a cherished memory from your past and thank God for his goodness that transcends time?

---

three

DECLUTTERING PHYSICAL AND MENTAL SPACE

[Elijah] looked, and there at his head was a cake baked on hot stones, and a jar of water. He ate and drank, and lay down again.

—1 Kings 19:6

LEARNING FROM PSYCHOLOGY

As we discussed in the previous chapter, busyness can undoubtedly detract from your ability to meaningfully engage with those around you. Interestingly, it might be not only the busyness of your own schedule but also the busyness of your environment that can make you less likely to help or engage meaningfully with those around you. Research that tries to isolate the environment's effect on helping behavior has explored how people interact when they are in settings with different population densities.

While it might be tempting to assume that people born and raised in cities are less helpful than people born and raised in small towns, research has shown that the busyness of your current environment matters more than where you are from.[1] In one series of studies looking at students in high-, medium-, and low-density dormitories, researchers demonstrated that the density of the environment affected many interpersonal measures, including trust and likability.[2] Additionally, density influenced how likely students were to help in a variety of different situations such as saving milk cartons for another student's art project or mailing a lost love letter. In low-density dorms, 90.6 percent of lost, stamped love letters (that had a recipient but not a return address), were put into a mailbox and eventually reached their end destination (the home of one of the researchers or their friends). The trend continued to decline as density increased, with only 77.4 percent of letters being placed in the mail in the medium density dorms and 63.6 percent of the letters in the high-density dorms. In other words, if you are packed in like sardines, you are less likely to help even when it costs you nothing.

While there are likely many factors at play, one proposed reason for this finding is what researchers call *cognitive overload.* A computer processing analogy explains this well. When you have too many programs open on your computer at one time, what happens? At best, everything is slow; at worst, the rainbow wheel of death sets in and you need to shut the whole thing down and restart. Why? Your computer cannot process everything at once. Brains are the same way—they begin to max out in super busy or chaotic environments because they are trying to process all the information at once.

While there are many different types of overload (social overload, information overload, choice overload, technology-based overload, etc.), the underlying principles are the same. With every person, piece of information, or choice that you encounter, there is an increased demand on your brain to sort through all the information and determine what is and what is not relevant and how you should respond.

According to cognitive load theory, people eventually hit a threshold where they need to reduce stimulation to conserve mental effort. Whether consciously or not, one common strategy is to disengage with whatever is taxing your mental space. For example, social overload is cited as a reason why people discontinue social media usage. Choice overload (having too many options) often results in indecision or ignoring the choice altogether. If you have ever felt completely overwhelmed by the absurd variety of pasta sauces at the grocery store, television shows available at the click of a button, or news about candidates before an election and have ultimately disengaged—failing to select a sauce, show, or senator—you are well acquainted with the consequences of overload.

In terms of happiness and satisfaction, less is more. This is, in part, because fewer options create less work for the brain. Having fewer choices to start with also minimizes potential regret over choices you did not make—whether it is something as simple as wishing you would have opted for original rather than rolling the dice with the garlic forward sauce or as complicated as choosing the political candidate that best aligns with your values.

In environments that are especially dense, becoming overloaded might result in tuning out the people around you in subtle (e.g., missing a request for help) or more obvious ways (e.g., walking around listening to music). While you may not always be able to choose the type of environment you live in (urban or rural), you can think more carefully about how you curate your own environments to reduce stimulation and fight your own tendencies to escape at the expense of being neighborly.

In a technologically driven environment, many people have more information at the tip of their fingers than can be contained in any actual environment, amplifying the potential for overload. Countless studies have documented the negative impacts of technology on relationships, and a massive global study conducted by Sapien Labs recently documented a strong link between mental health and the age someone received their first cell phone (yes, on average, the longer you wait the better).[3] A suggestion to spend less time on your phone to be a better neighbor to those around you is thus unlikely to feel revolutionary. But it might serve you well to pay more attention to your unique threshold.

We do not all overload at the same point. Some of us have a higher tolerance. Our set points are a product of a variety of biological (e.g., baseline levels of cortisol and sympathetic nervous system activity), psychological (e.g., personality, trauma), and sociocultural (e.g., being raised in high-density, high-stimulus environments) factors. Becoming aware of your own threshold can help you avoid situations in which you are physically less capable of acting neighborly to strangers (or even with basic kindness to friends or loved ones), and also to strategically engage with coping strategies when overstimulating situations cannot be avoided.

Beyond understanding our own tipping points, it is also worthwhile to acknowledge that reducing the distractions or stimulation in your environment might take more effort and foresight than you initially anticipate. For example, a well-intentioned individual might insightfully acknowledge that they have a low threshold for stimulation and easily become cognitively overloaded. This may lead them to take valuable steps to change their environment—silencing their cell phone or removing some of the notifications that they typically receive. This is a great first step, but psychological research suggests that it is unlikely to be enough, especially if the goal is to foster relationships and connection with others. Why? Because relationships suffer in the mere presence of technological devices. This has been demonstrated in instances when a phone is simply on the table—even if it doesn't belong to anyone![4]

In other words, the problem is not simply that people ignore each other or experience disruptions in the flow of social interactions because they are (rudely) paying attention to their phones (although this happens a lot too). Instead, the issue psychological research highlights is that human brains cannot easily turn off the constant monitoring of a phone or technological device. At any moment your brain thinks you might need to be ready for the "ding," and so you remain on guard and prepared for that unexpected event, which limits your ability to be fully present in the moment.

In one demonstration of this, researchers brought participants into the laboratory and paired them up so that they would be able to have a ten-minute conversation with someone they didn't know. Specifically, participants were prompted to discuss something interesting that happened to them in the past month. Half of the pairs were assigned to a "no phone" condition, in which they sat at a table that had a small pen and paper notebook placed on the table. The other half were assigned to a "phone" condition where a nondescript phone was placed on the table where they were seated.

After the conversation, the researchers assessed several indicators of the quality of the interaction and the social connection the pairs experienced. The results of two studies demonstrated that the mere presence of a random mobile phone on a table where participants sat to have a conversation reduced perceptions of relationship quality, including measures of closeness, trust, and empathic concern. The researchers did not find any evidence to suggest that participants were aware that the presence of the phone detracted from their interactions. In other words, even when you are convinced a phone is not distracting you, there appears to be a measurable (and negative) impact on the quality of your interactions, likely because you're nonconsciously monitoring the phone, which is siphoning some of your mental space.

An extension of this work explored whether similar findings would be seen outside of a laboratory, when people were interacting with those in their actual social circles. Identifying the phenomenon dubbed the *iPhone effect*, this study demonstrated that as relationship closeness increased, so did the negative consequences of having a mobile phone present.[5] Another way of saying this is that having a phone present during conversations may hurt your closest relationships the most. In one demonstration of this, the phones belonged to the participants, but they did not need to be used to have negative effects. The researchers simply determined if the phones were visibly present (on a table or in someone's hand) at any point during the ten-minute interaction. For the pairs where at least one phone was present, people reported feeling measurably less empathic concern for the individual they were interacting with.[6] Empathy (as we will learn) is a critical component for healthy relationships and a necessary precursor for most types of helping behaviors. It is an emotional ingredient we cannot afford to lose if our goal is to love others better.

Psych Summary: Just like being in a hurry makes you less likely to love your neighbors well, so does being overstimulated. This overstimulation is not always consciously felt, but it affects your ability to engage with others nonetheless. What is even more tricky is that your brain can become overloaded by things that are not even yours (e.g., someone else's cell phone) and things that seem inconsequential (e.g., the number of pasta sauces you have to pick from before making spaghetti). In a capitalistic and technology-driven society, it requires an incredible amount of diligence to curate your environment and your time in such a way that you are not always overloaded to the point of being unable to engage with those whom God places in your path.

THINKING THEOLOGICALLY

> But he [Elijah] himself went a day's journey into the wilderness, and came and sat down under a solitary broom tree. He asked that he might die: "It is enough; now, O Lord, take away my life, for I am no better than my ancestors." Then he lay down under the broom tree and fell asleep. Suddenly an angel touched him and said to him, "Get up and eat." He looked, and there at his head was a cake baked on hot stones, and a jar of water. He ate and drank, and lay down again. The angel of the Lord came a second time, touched him, and said, "Get up and eat, otherwise the journey will be too much for you." He got up, and ate and drank; then he went in the

> strength of that food forty days and forty nights to Horeb the mount of God. At that place he came to a cave, and spent the night there.
>
> Then the word of the Lord came to him, saying, "What are you doing here, Elijah?" He answered, "I have been very zealous for the Lord, the God of hosts; for the Israelites have forsaken your covenant, thrown down your altars, and killed your prophets with the sword. I alone am left, and they are seeking my life, to take it away."
>
> —1 Kings 19:4-10

In this story, Elijah is a perfect model of the overload hypothesis. For context, go back and read 1 Kings 18-19. Elijah is in an epic battle with the 450 prophets of Baal to prove who is the true God. Elijah challenges the king, Ahab, to invite everyone in Israel to see whether Baal or Elijah's God will light the fire to burn the ox that was sacrificed by each side. After the prayers of the prophets of Baal fail to ignite their sacrifice, Elijah constructs a new altar and has water dumped on his sacrifice. He prays to the God of Israel, who sends fire that consumes the sacrifice, the altar made of stones, and all of the water on and around the altar—lots of action. Everyone who witnesses this converts, shouting, "The Lord indeed is God!" (1 Kings 18:39). After he wins the showdown, Elijah is involved in a lot of intense tasks. After having the prophets of Baal killed, he hikes to the top of a mountain and sends his servant to run to look toward the sea seven times until he sees a cloud the size of a hand coming out of the sea, which signals the end of a three-year drought. When Jezebel hears that the prophets of Baal have been killed, she threatens to kill Elijah by the following day. Elijah flees to Beersheba, going into the desert, where he collapses from exhaustion under a broom bush.

More is asked of him than he is capable of, and finally he says, "It is enough now, O Lord." Enough already! Elijah is spent. So he walks out into the wilderness to get some space. He takes a nap, and an angel offers him a snack and some water. Then he is sent out on a forty-day wilderness retreat.

These are strange details to include in a biblical text, and yet, they seem to point to the same insights as the overload hypothesis and research about the value of spending time in a less socially dense area. The command to love is challenging because sometimes, more is asked of us than we expect or think we are capable of. This can lead us to feeling overwhelmed.

Some, like Elijah, are called to exceptional circumstances. For him, the call was to act as a diplomat between nations as God's representative. Most of us are not called to this level of demand from others (entire nations). Most of us are in our homes and jobs, doing the best we can, and scrolling on our phone can deceptively feel like a restful distraction from a world teeming with endless needs. Spoiler: scrolling actually contributes to overload. If we do manage to silence our phones and pay attention, listening to the pain and needs of our neighbors may begin to feel overwhelming. And yet, we know that we are not called to ignore the problems of this world, but to listen closely and to love anyway.

Glennon Doyle, a writer and podcaster, wrote in a 2016 blog, "There is no such thing as other people's children."[7] The assumption in this is that we should love each child as if they were our own. The people we would donate a kidney for, defend in court, offer a ride to the airport, volunteer to teach to read at school—this is the kind of relationship we should have with everyone. And yet, this feels impossible, like living this way would lead us to be just one more case study of the overload hypothesis.

Perhaps you have heard of the children's book titled *Yes Day!* which was also made into a movie where Jennifer Garner is the darling mom. The premise of the book is that the parents say yes to any request made by the child. In the movie, this results in the parents reconnecting with their kids and embracing their own playful inner child. In real life this sounds like a nightmare. Would our kids ask for a trip to Disneyland, a new virtual reality headset, or cake for dinner? It seems to set kids up for disappointment and result in something more like a "My-mom-is-no-fun Day" instead of a "Yes Day!"

Well, when Katie's son brought home his own fill-in-the-blanks *Yes Day!* book, it was filled with sweet requests like, "Can I have pizza for breakfast?" and "Can we watch a movie together after school?" and "Can I eat only blueberries for dinner?" What is telling in this is not that the kids were actually pretty reasonable (which they were, for the most part), but rather the parental fear, or maybe just the human fear, that if we open ourselves up to the infinite possibility of requests from another person, they might ask for more than we are capable of giving . . . and then we will feel bad, because we do not want to disappoint anyone. But what if we were to hold our fears at bay and invite the infinite possibility of demands from others while not succumbing to overload. Are we even capable of this kind of openness? And if we are, how do we sustain loving our neighbors with a full and open heart?

In her book *How to Do Nothing: Resisting the Attention Economy*, art professor Jenny Odell holds up Thomas Merton as an exemplar of someone who mastered the art of giving his attention to good, worthy things rather than letting the world distract him into the busy numbness of daily interruptions. He was a master at avoiding overload (or at least knowing when to retreat when overloaded) *and* he was a master at retreat, which Odell recognizes as the subversive resistance to participating in the ways of the world. Odell's work is new, and yet rings with deep, age-old truths. Odell critiques what she calls the "attention economy," claiming that social media, the constant pings from our phone, and the idol of busyness have distracted us and led us to believe that a life full of distractions is meaningful and a good way to spend our time.[8] And yet, we know that it is our relationships and our contributions to the lives of others that make a meaningful life.

Dietrich Bonhoeffer wrote an entire book about this dynamic, called *Life Together*. We humans need time alone, to be present to ourselves, and time together, to be present to others. We give and receive in both spaces. His main point is that we all need both, and yet all of us are slightly inclined toward one and avoid the other. What research shows us is that this balance is needed to help us love our neighbors better. When we open ourselves up to the needs and requests of others, we do run up against our human limits, and like Elijah, we need time for a retreat, a nap, and a snack. In this state, however, we can also see that when we are fully present with others (aware of the density of our community, aware of our occasional need for space) we can love our neighbors in ways that we had not, perhaps, otherwise imagined we were capable of.

The world of theology uses the term *supererogation* to describe the reality that sometimes we take responsibility for more than is expected of us—when we go "beyond the call of duty" in ways that are morally good, true, and beautiful. All of us, at times, find ourselves in scenarios where we feel that the Holy Spirit is calling us to do more, to intervene, to give or lead in ways that seem beyond what is expected of us—and miraculously, by the power of the Holy Spirit, we are able to do it. These are amazing moments, when you can see the power of God at work in your life, but even then, like Elijah, we need to retreat, to rest.

Sometimes loving our neighbors is simple and not very demanding. But sometimes loving our neighbor is very demanding, and we may feel overwhelmed by the infinite (and likely very reasonable) needs of our neighbors. If we understand the overload hypothesis, we can recognize our need for a snack and a nap, and wake up refreshed and ready to love.

LIVING FAITHFULLY

Consider what types of overload are most present in your day.

- Are your days socially dense, filled by constantly answering customer questions, or leading a large classroom packed with students?

- Do you have a constant stream of meetings, classes back-to-back, or perhaps a lot of your day is spent in a home that is filled with high-energy humans?
- Do you live in a dense environment where you see into your neighbor's bathroom from your living room window, or would you only see your neighbors when they are out shoveling their driveway or mowing their lawn?
- Are your days informationally dense, sorting through thousands of pieces of data, litigation paperwork, or complex emails?

What do you do to escape or minimize the overload? Are you engaging in quiet moments of solitude, or do you lock yourself in the bathroom for a few moments on your phone? One danger is that it can be easy to accidentally replace one form of overload for another (cyber overload). Psychology research demonstrates that certain activities are far more effective at countering overload than others (hint: they very rarely include screens). Here are some ideas to reduce cognitive overload and create small moments of restoration.

One easy change is to consider ways to reduce sensory input.

- Turn down the lights.
- Turn off the radio in your car.
- Go for a walk without listening to music.
- Turn off your phone.

Another option is to consider emotional rest. This includes both opportunities to feel and process our emotions and decisions to disengage from emotionally draining situations and engage in emotionally fulfilling ones.

- Take a break from the endless cycles of bad news.
- Say no to an event that will be emotionally draining.

- Say yes to something just because you know it will feel good or bring you joy (cuddling babies or puppies anyone?).
- Journal your emotions.
- Let yourself cry, like really cry.
- Engage in a form of body movement that requires your full attention (e.g., a complicated Zumba or karate class) so that your mind is less likely to wander back to the social or emotional knots you are trying to mentally untangle.

Look at the settings on your phone and computer. Take out your phone or computer, go into your settings, and prayerfully consider how these might be turned off or on to help you to be present to those whom you spend the day with.

- What notifications can be turned off or silenced?
- What "reminders" are actually distractions and which ones actually help you to be present?
- How many red notification circles on your phone, watch, or computer can you turn off so that when you look at it, you don't end up spending more time than you originally intended?
- Could you set a timer for something so that in the meanwhile, you can put your phone away and be present to the people you are with?

Consider how you carry your phone or the watch that you wear.

- Experiment for a day with placing it in a purse or backpack rather than a pocket to see how this physical distance might allow you to offer the gift of your attention throughout the day to those whom God is calling you to notice.
- Have you noticed how enjoyable it is to spend time with someone who doesn't check their phone while you are together? Maybe you can be that friend who is able to give their

full attention, and maybe even begin to hear cries of the oppressed that we are all too often too distracted to hear.

What is your version of Elijah's nap, snack, and retreat?

- Is there a place where you can breathe deeply and say, "When I am here, I am able to be the person that I want to be." Once you figure out where that place is, find ways to spend more time there.
- Can you find time to slowly peel an orange, enjoying its smell and the spray from the rind on your hands as you peel it before you eat it, one section at a time? Are you able to slow down enough to notice what your body needs and then simply meet that need with a warm cup of tea or the sweet crunch of an apple?
- Is there a small green space or a beautiful yard near where you spend your days that you could take a short walk to, leaving your phone in your home or office, just to move your body and enjoy a short time of connecting with environmental beauty (and disconnecting from technology)?
- Could you create a new bedtime ritual of crawling into bed early without your phone, planning to just let your mind wander for ten minutes before falling asleep?

four

ASSUMING RESPONSIBILITY, EVEN WHEN IT'S NOT YOUR FAULT

"Did I conceive all these people? Did I give birth to them?"

—Numbers 11:12

LEARNING FROM PSYCHOLOGY

Have you ever personally witnessed an emergency or a time when another individual was in sudden or immediate need of help? Take a moment to try to isolate one such event in your memory. If you cannot think of an emergency, then think of a time that stands out in your mind when you decided not to help someone who was in need or asked you for help. After identifying an event, please unpack it using the prompts below.

Briefly describe the scenario:

My response: I helped or I did not help (circle one).

Reasons for my response (my action or inaction):

1.

2.

3.

4.

5.

Now take a quick look over your list. Our guess is whether or not you helped, you mentioned something about (1) who the person was and how they were (or were not) connected to you, (2) your own sense of (in)competence, whether you felt like you knew what to do or how to help, and/or (3) a sense of responsibility to help—this may range significantly from a sense that the Spirit was calling you to help to your sense of professional identity. For example, if you are a nurse or a doctor, your knowledge and profession may create a deep sense of responsibility to help those in medical emergencies (even when you are not at work). Likely, far fewer of you wrote anything about how many people were around to witness the emergency or the person in need of help. How many people are around may not be one of the first things on our mind when trying to decide if or how we will intervene. But according to social psychological research, it is nonetheless a prominent factor driving your behavior.

Were you in a large crowd or were you one of a few people (or perhaps even the only person) to witness the emergency? If the former is true, then your decision to help was driven, in large part, by your connection to the person in need and your awareness about how to help. If you were the only one, you likely stepped in even with no connection to the individual in need, and perhaps even in the absence of knowing how to help. A well-established psychological phenomenon, known as the *bystander effect*, documents this by showing how people are not only more likely to help, but also quicker to help if there are fewer people around.

One of the most famous studies of the bystander effect staged a (fake) emergency to see if participants would get up and help a man they believed to be having a stroke. The experiment took place in a large room full of cubicles. Participants were placed in a single cubicle and given a headset to speak with other participants (presumably seated in other cubicles throughout the large room). Participants believed that they were either one of two participants in the study (the "no other bystander" condition), one of three participants in the study (the "one other bystander" condition) or one of five participants in the study (the "multiple bystander" condition). After the initial engagements, one of the participants (actually a researcher feigning as a participant) pretended to have a stroke. The real participant could hear the emergency unfold over their headset. Researchers were interested to observe two outcomes: (1) if the real participant would get up to look for the individual or seek some sort of assistance, and (2) how long it would take the participant to respond.

What they found was that when participants believed they were the only other person in the study (and thus the only one who could hear the emergency and knew the man was in need of help), 100 percent of the participants acted within the first three minutes (85 percent responded in just over sixty seconds by the time the alleged stroke victim's voice was no longer heard).

In the "one other bystander" condition, where participants believed one other participant could hear the emergency, they were less likely to help at all, and slower to respond. In this condition, only 80 percent responded at all, and just over 60 percent responded within the first seventy seconds.

This trend amplified in the "multiple bystander" condition, where helping never reached more than 60 percent and a meager 30 percent helped in the first seventy seconds.

There are several notable takeaways from this study. First, a greater number of people present to witness an emergency decreases the likelihood that any one person will help and makes people slower to respond or provide any form of aid.[1] Second, the reductions in helpfulness cannot be attributed to seeing (or otherwise knowing) that another person had already stepped in to help. In the study, there was never an indicator that the person in need was ever attended to.

What is going on here? Researchers suggest this phenomenon is evidence of a *diffusion of responsibility*. Put simply, when multiple people are present, no one person feels like it is *their* responsibility to do something. We might think, Who am I to step up and intervene? Surely someone else will. Or, There must be a doctor or someone else here far more qualified to help than I am. I wouldn't even know how to help. This cognitive spiral moves us further from feeling personally responsible to help.

One caveat to this diffusion is the roles we have in different environments. If you happen to be a doctor or a nurse, you likely will not experience this same diffusion in a medical emergency. Additionally, the role you play in a particular environment will affect your likelihood of helping. In one high school re-creation of the bystander effect, a student pretended to faint in the hall when students were changing classes. A camera was surreptitiously placed to film the individual and all passersby. Tens of individuals walked past the one collapsed on the floor, until a teacher came along, noticed the collapsed student, and intervened, only to thankfully realize that the fainting was staged for a psychology class project. Here, the teacher had a unique role whereby they likely felt more responsible for the well-being of the students in the school and thus were quick to respond even though there were so many other people present.

Even if we do not have prominent roles in a particular place, research suggests that being informed of the bystander effect can significantly enhance the likelihood of helping. So, now you know. You are welcome to begin assuming responsibility.

It can also be helpful to teach people to counter the narrative that "someone else has probably already helped" by telling yourself, If I don't help, no one else will. This may or may not be true for your specific situation, but at the very least, it could help to alleviate the time delays in responding. Very little can go wrong if too many people try to help (which is unlikely anyway) because it simply creates opportunities to identify the people with the greatest expertise to help. Where we get into trouble is when everyone assumes someone else will, and in reality no one helps at all. In real-life scenarios, forgoing this hesitation in an emergency could make a significant difference in the life and well-being of another person.

A related series of studies put a varied number of participants, one to twelve, in a room to complete a lengthy questionnaire. While participants were completing the questionnaire, researchers pumped the room with smoke. They were interested to see if anyone would get up and alert a researcher about the smoke. Video recordings of these experiments reveal an incredibly interesting dynamic. Participants clearly notice the smoke. You can see them looking at it, and then looking around to their peers to see if anyone else looks perturbed or panicked. Noticing no other individuals who seem concerned, most participants carry on filling out the questionnaire in the smoke-filled room.

Here, the bystander effect meets another phenomenon researchers refer to as *pluralistic ignorance*. Essentially, people misinterpret other people's lack of overt responses as an indication that they do not feel concerned about what is happening. Because we are social creatures, we look to others to tell us how we should feel about things. Think of a baby who bumps their head lightly and then looks to the caregiver. If the caregiver smiles, the baby smiles, if they look horrified, the baby will often burst into tears. Navigating uncertainty in social environments follows a similar process—we look to others for cues about how concerned (or unconcerned) we should be. This is a reason to make your concerns known and to ask directly about whether or not others are experiencing concern.

Another example of this is when something sexist or racist happens and no one says anything. The nonresponse can communicate to others that sexist or racist comments or actions are okay. The problem is our assumptions about how others feel are often wrong, and the chances that we will catch someone else's eye at the immediate moment we are noticing the smoke or cringing at the comment is relatively small.

All these psychological phenomena affect helping because they disrupt primary requirements for helping. If you remember the stages of helping laid out in chapter 2, you remember that noticing an event is critical for helping to occur. Here the event is clearly noticed, but pluralistic ignorance can keep us from identifying the event as an emergency (step 2), and diffusion of responsibility can keep us from assuming personal responsibility to respond (step 3).

Arguably, an even larger problem is that we are looking to other people to tell us how to act or feel in the first place instead of asking what a faithful response is. Can you imagine if the good Samaritan had simply followed the cues of the others who passed by the person in need of help? God calls us to be in the world, but not of it. We should be breaking norms, not reinforcing them. Our response to people who need help, who are being verbally degraded, or who are in a crisis should be a disruptive witness that causes people to ask, "What motivated you to respond differently than everyone else?"

Psych Summary: Being aware of factors that make us less likely to help, such as the number of people present in an emergency, can help us fight our own tendency to step back and assume others will do the helping. As Christians, it is our personal responsibility to love our neighbors as ourselves, not to simply assume that other people will love our neighbors. The psychology research reminds us to take responsibility, even when it isn't our fault or there are a lot of other people who could do it. Doing so ensures that those who are hurting (both emotionally and physically) receive the help they need quickly.

THINKING THEOLOGICALLY

> So Moses said to the Lord, "Why have you treated your servant so badly? Why have I not found favor in your sight, that you lay the burden of all these people on me? Did I conceive all these people? Did I give birth to them, that you should say to me, 'Carry them in your bosom, as a nurse carries a sucking child,' to the land that you promised on oath to their ancestors? Where am I to get meat to give to all these people? For they come weeping to me and say, 'Give us meat to eat!' I am not able to carry all these people alone, for they are too heavy for me. If this is the way you are going to treat me, put me to death at once—if I have found favor in your sight—and do not let me see my misery."
>
> —Numbers 11:11–15

After successfully fleeing enslavement, the Hebrew people are wandering in the desert, eating manna, and feeling nostalgic about the fish, cucumbers, melons, leeks, onions, and garlic that they used to eat (Num. 11:1–10). The complaining wanderers get a lot of attention in sermons and Sunday school lessons. Anyone who has been on a vacation with children who want to go home and play with their friends knows how Moses felt. In this passage it is clear that Moses feels like a parent with children who complain, but he also feels like he has been unfairly burdened with caring for people he does not want to be responsible for.

In response to their complaints, Moses turns to God and says, "These aren't my kids! I didn't birth them. If they are hungry, that is your responsibility, not mine!" And not only that, he tells God that if God is going to make it his responsibility, he would rather die. "Put me to death at once," Moses says to God (Num. 11:15). His frustration, exasperation, and annoyance are deep. As a leader, Moses has seen it all, from being adopted into a royal family, seeing his people enslaved, watching a murder, being weighed down with the guilt of killing someone himself, living through the plagues, leading people through a sea while being chased by an army, and now the people he has freed are not really free, but dependent on him, and to top it off, they are complaining. Despite his initial resistance, Moses shows us how to take responsibility, even when they are not "your kids" and you are tired of *these* people.

This is not the first time Moses is asked to take responsibility. When Moses meets God in the burning bush (he is running away from responsibility), he tells God to find someone else, someone more qualified, someone who is a better public speaker. Both at the burning bush and in the desert we see that despite his valid arguments, he ultimately takes responsibility.

What if God is calling each of us to be like Moses in the places where we live? It is clear from the various stories of Moses that he is not called to take responsibility because he is the most qualified or the best public speaker, but because he is the one who is in that particular place at that particular time. Similar to participants in the psychological studies, Moses goes through the pattern of thinking that this is someone else's responsibility, or surely there is someone who is more qualified to be a leader during this crisis.

What if we start thinking that, wherever we are, this is the exact place and time that God has called us, and that God wants to work through us to help those we encounter. We can recognize the insecurities and inner voices that tell us to shirk responsibility, and instead boldly take responsibility beyond what we think we are capable of and beyond what others expect of us. And we can do this, not just because it's the right thing to do, but because the command to love is a call to take up responsibility for the well-being of others. It can be really uncomfortable to do this because our society trains us to keep boundaries and not get involved in other people's business. We need to rebelliously resist this insipid pressure to conform.

LIVING FAITHFULLY

Many examples for the bystander effect have to do with emergency situations. To respond differently in a future emergency, you might begin by imagining the places you frequently go, and consider how you might think, "I am here, so I'll help."

Most of us do not encounter emergencies daily, but that does not mean we cannot act in helpful ways by claiming responsibility. Imagine you are Moses: Who is in your world right now that you might wish you did not have responsibility for? What would it look like for you to stop making assumptions that another person will help and start telling yourself, "If I don't help, no one else will."

Taking responsibility can be small, like picking up the trash in your neighborhood or clearing the broken bottle off the sidewalk at the park. Just because you didn't make the mess doesn't mean you can't take responsibility for helping to clean it up. Channel Miller talks about striving to keep her own little corner of the world beautiful. As someone who bravely navigated the public trauma of sexual assault on Stanford University's campus, Miller talks about this focus as something that helps to counter her own past trauma and accompanying overwhelm.[2]

When you think about your daily routine map from chapter 1, what problem or struggle do you pass by or encounter every day:

- Is there a section of the sidewalk that has trash that needs to be picked up?
- Do you have a neighbor who is recently widowed, who would love a visit?

- Do you have a friend who gossips, or makes racist jokes in ways that make you uncomfortable? What would it look like to speak up?
- Is there someone in the LGBTQ community in your circles who could use someone just to tell them, "I am glad that we are friends"?
- Do you have a neighbor with a kid with disabilities who could use a friend to talk with, or perhaps you could spend some time enjoying their kid and telling the parent what you like about them?
- Is there someone at work who is new or seems lonely that you could ask to have lunch with you?
- Could you help one of your neighbors remove the graffiti from their fence?
- Do you have an older neighbor who would enjoy a ride with you to the grocery store?

Taking responsibility when you notice something is a simple yet profound way you can love your neighbors.

part two

WHEN THOUGHTS AND FEELINGS GET IN THE WAY OF LOVING YOUR NEIGHBOR

five

GIVING OTHERS THE BENEFIT OF THE DOUBT

I do not understand my own actions. For I do not do what I want, but I do the very thing I hate.

—Romans 7:15

LEARNING FROM PSYCHOLOGY

Take a moment to think about a recent situation when someone was rude to you. Describe it here.

Now, consider the story you are telling yourself about why the person treated you the way they did. If you had to explain the why behind their behavior, what would you say? Be honest: What thoughts about the person's behavior are most commonly running through your mind? Write them below.

Consider the severity of the action you identified. Maybe the person blew you off when you said hello, wrote a curt text message in response to a long, heartfelt bid for connection, or said something genuinely cruel. Whatever it is, the fact that it sprang to mind and that you took the time to write it down is a strong signal that the behavior hurt you. We are also willing to bet that you have spent some time searching for an explanation as to why the person did or said what they did. Likely, the first explanation that came to mind is not your most generous or grace-filled explanation. It probably is not an explanation that is going to help you be neighborly to that person in the future. To the contrary, it is probably an explanation that fuels your anger toward that person. So, let's unpack your options and the associated consequences of how you answer that all-too-familiar question, Why would they do that to me?

According to *attribution theory*, our attempts to understand the behavior of others can lead us to draw one of two conclusions. Either they were in a challenging situation (*situational attribution*) or they behaved that way because of their disposition (*dispositional attribution*). A situational attribution focuses on the circumstances (or situations) someone was experiencing at the time of the behavior. For example, you might think, "They did not send me a long thoughtful text back because that was the same day their whole family came down with a stomach bug." A dispositional attribution, on the other hand, explains someone's behavior in terms of their character or who they are as a person. An example of this is to think, "They did not send me a long thoughtful text back because they are cold or overly self-involved" (their disposition).

It is clear from the examples that when we attribute someone's behavior to their disposition, it can hurt our relationships because we label them with negative traits instead of assuming that outside circumstances led to their behavior. Unfortunately, our brains spontaneously jump to dispositional explanations when we try to understand the why behind another person's unhelpful, unimpressive, or unpleasant actions. Why was this student late for class? Because they are disrespectful. Why did my coworker give a sloppy work presentation? Because they are lazy. Why did my brother forget my birthday? Because he is self-absorbed. Why is a child not following the rules? Because they are disobedient. Dispositional explanations erode our perceptions of another person's competence and character. They are also biased.

How are dispositional attributions biased? From a psychological perspective, they are biased because they are not applied equally. Let's see if we can pinpoint this together.

Take a moment to think about a recent situation when you were rude to someone else. Maybe it was something relatively subtle, or a genuinely terrible thing you did. Name the action and then try to explain why you did what you did.

We suspect that most (if not all) of you came up with at least one and possibly many situational factors that helped you explain your behavior. I snapped at my partner, forgot to submit my homework, made a careless mistake because I . . . was exhausted from a long day at work, got caught up caring for a friend going through a difficult breakup, was distracted by news of a sick family member. The lists of circumstantial evidence could go on and on. It is unlikely that you listed dispositional reasons—I am a careless person, I am an angry person, I don't love my partner, etc.

Do you see the difference? We can appreciate with great clarity the extent to which situations and circumstances affect our own negative behavior. Yet, we have a blind spot when it comes to seeing how situations affect other people's negative behaviors. This is not our "fault," so to speak, and it happens to us all. At the same time, when we know better, we can do better.

Psychologists refer to this asymmetry in how we explain our own and other people's behaviors as the *fundamental attribution error*. It is a natural bias that stems from the fact that every person has limited knowledge of other people's experiences. Your partner may have had a terrible day, but you were not there, you did not see it. All you *see* is the disgruntled look you get when you ask for a favor. It is impossible to know what you do not see or experience, unless you ask the right questions or someone takes the initiative to explain.

The fundamental attribution error is important for many reasons. The more we see others as incapable, unkind, or just "not good" people, the less likely we are to engage in meaningful interactions with them. Not only does this lack of engagement ensure that our beliefs about the other will remain fixed (there will be an absence of positive information to counter our negative perceptions), but it also changes the way we think about whether or not they are worthy of being helped, or even just treated with common dignity.

From a theological perspective, there is much to contest about the idea that someone is or is not worthy of these things, but the reality from a psychological standpoint is that perceptions of worthiness are a part of the (often nonconscious) mental calculation that changes the likelihood that we will help or be kind to another person in need.

Unfortunately, the fundamental attribution error is just the tip of the iceberg. The malleability of our beliefs about other people's worthiness is always problematic. While we are called to see that all humans are created in the image of God and as such have innate (and consistent) worth and value, psychology exposes how quickly our perceptions of other people's worth fluctuates. One of the most striking demonstrations of this is seen when we are trying to make sense, not of why people are mean to us, but rather why bad things happen to good people.

How we process events as serious as sexual assault or as benign as who loses a coin toss are shaped by our own fear of experiencing similar fates. We want to believe that those things could never happen to us and so we begin to create explanations for the negative outcomes that blame the person who is experiencing the harm or loss. This insidious form of victim blaming can be explained, in part, by the fact that our brains are trying to protect us and help us feel safe in the world. We need to believe that we will not end up in situations or circumstances that are undesirable or unfavorable. We want to believe, "That will not happen to me as long as I do all the 'right' things and make the 'right' choices." This is our brain creating the illusion of safety and control.

Psychologists aptly refer to this as *blaming the victim*, and we are more likely to do it the more tightly we hold to the belief that the world is a fair and just place. These personal beliefs combined with a desire to explain or understand negative events give rise to the *just-world phenomenon*. This is one of the most sinister concepts in all of social psychology because instead of accepting that the world is not just and doing what we can to actively counter that injustice, people often create the illusion of justice in their own minds by blaming others for negative fates that are often largely (if not entirely) beyond their control.

If you have ever had someone tell you that it was your fault that your bike (or anything else) was stolen, you may have gotten a small taste of what it is like to be on the receiving end of victim blaming. If you have ever snarkily thought "What goes around comes around," you have subscribed (at least momentarily) to the belief in a just world where wrongs are eventually "righted" or repaid. Now that we are familiar with the concepts, let's look at how these phenomena play out in scientific research.

One of the most powerful social psychology experiments to demonstrate victim blaming asks participants to read a simple interaction between a man and a woman and then to rate the woman's behavior on a number of factors.[1] In particular, things like how flirtatious she was being or how inappropriate she acted. All the participants read the exact same, relatively bland, scenario. Importantly, however, half were given one additional piece of information. They were told that shortly after the interaction the woman was sexually assaulted by the man. Researchers then looked to see if the judgments about the woman's behavior were different between the two groups.

Consistent with the phenomenon of victim blaming, what the researchers found was that those who were told about the eventual sexual assault judged the woman's behavior to be less appropriate than those who were not given the additional information. Take that in for a moment. The exact same behaviors are judged differently after a negative outcome is known. This study and others like it hold crucial lessons for how quickly and unfairly people blame the victims of sexual assault. This type of victim blaming is devastatingly consequential for the mental health and well-being of those who have been assaulted. It also undermines the process of accountability for the assaulter.

A similar process of victim blaming plays out in many other contexts, including the rewards that are associated with hard work. In one experiment, participants were brought into a lab to observe workers and rate their performance. Unbeknownst to the participants, the workers were a part of the experiment. They both were trained to work equally hard and to be equally productive during the time that they were observed. As the observation period ended, the experimenter came in and told the workers that unfortunately they only had enough money to pay one of them. To decide who would get the money, the researcher would flip a coin. The worker who won the coin toss got paid, and the other walked away empty handed.

Participants who observed the work and payment process play out were then asked to do a performance evaluation of sorts where they rate the two workers on a variety of dimensions. Interestingly, although both workers had worked equally hard and produced the same amount, participants rated the one who had won the coin toss as more productive and a harder worker. Why? Because their brains were trying to find a way to justify, or make sense out of, what just happened. Either this is an obvious injustice, which is uncomfortable to accept, or maybe, just maybe, the person who won the coin flip had actually worked just a little bit harder. Because the process is a nonconscious one, people have no idea they are doing it. They walk away believing that the workers got what they deserved.

It is unsettling for most people to really think about how much of their life is beyond their control. Many outcomes and occurrences come down to the equivalent of a coin flip, the luck of the draw, or simply being in the wrong place at the wrong time. Accepting this is psychologically unnerving because it creates a heightened awareness of a lack of control. Without control, people feel vulnerable. Instead of working to accept this vulnerability, it is often easier to blame others for the bad things that happen to them and maintain the belief that you can avoid the same unfortunate fate if you do all the right things (unlike "them").

If we tell ourselves these false (and harmful) stories that a woman was sexually assaulted because she was overly flirtatious or that a person was paid less because they did not work as hard, then we feel less vulnerable. We believe if we are more careful about how we interact with people or go out of our way to work harder than someone else, we will not incur similarly traumatic or unfair fates. It makes us feel better to think that good things happen to "good" people who act "good" and make "good" choices. And bad things happen to "bad" people who act "bad" or make "bad" choices.

At the core, we are inclined to want to believe that the world is fair. Of course, we all know that good things can happen to "bad" people and bad things can happen to "good" people, but the reality of this terrifies us. We want to believe that as long as we are "good" we will stay safe and good things will happen to us in return. The outcome of this is that when we look at folks in negative situations, we begin to weave stories about their personalities and their choices that help us mentally justify how they got to where they are and assure ourselves that we could never end up in the same place. The good news is we have an innate longing for justice. The bad news is we live in an unjust world. We can use our longing to participate in the work of God in the world, or we can use it to blame hurting people who, like us, are all God's children.

It is hard to overstate the real-world consequences of victim blaming and the just-world phenomenon. This sneaky mental math is present when we wrestle with really difficult questions about poverty, pain, loss, inequality, and injustice of every kind. And the tendency to fall prey to this phenomenon is the strongest for people who have grown up in highly individualistic cultures, like the United States, where people generally believe that individuals are both in charge of and responsible for their own fates.

Wondering if you are at higher risk for leveraging the just-world phenomenon against others no matter how unintentionally? A good friend and colleague who recently wrote a textbook about cross-cultural psychology,[2] Dr. Paul Youngbin Kim, shared some of Dr. Wing-Sue's research that could help. The findings suggest that endorsing statements like "You only have yourself to blame if things go wrong in this world" is a strong indicator that you have internalized an individualistic approach to processing events.[3] Another narrative that may feel familiar to people in the United States is the mentality of "pulling yourself up by your bootstraps." While there is nothing wrong with hard work or taking personal responsibility (indeed God calls us to these things, especially when it comes to helping others), we should also be wary of the potential consequences if these perspectives are unchecked or unbalanced. When cultures and environments place a disproportionate emphasis on individual control and autonomy, unhelpful (and often harmful) victim blaming becomes more likely. These cultures are also the ones where people feel most alone in their failures and are most discouraged when their hard work does not pay off in the way it "should."

The flip side of too much blame is too much praise. The very same environments that place too much emphasis on personal responsibility when things go wrong can also fuel pride and unhealthy self-sufficiency when things go "right." These environments can lead to destructive competition and greed by propagating the belief that any success (including our own) is solely a result of hard work or personal effort, without recognizing the elements of luck, financial resources, teamwork, social capital, or countless other factors that facilitated the success. Acknowledging that different cultures view questions of responsibility through different lenses (people and their fates are independent vs. interdependent) presents us with an opportunity to explore when the real-world consequences of these beliefs are (and are not) in line with Jesus's teachings.

Let's consider, for example, the intersection of individualistic perspectives and the just-world phenomenon on the increasing rates of homelessness in the United States. In trying to make sense of why some individuals have housing and others do not, it is common to identify dispositional (rather than situational) explanations. What might some of those explanations be? You can note any potential dispositional explanations whether you agree with them or not.

DISPOSITIONAL EXPLANATIONS FOR HOMELESSNESS:

"These people are homeless because they are . . ."

1.

2.

3.

4.

Now, take a moment to explore situational explanations, instead. Make a list of factors related to luck or circumstance that could contribute to folks' being unhoused. You can note any potential situational explanations whether you agree with them or not.

SITUATIONAL EXPLANATIONS FOR HOMELESSNESS:

"These people are homeless because of . . . circumstances."

1.

2.

3.

4.

When students in our classes complete this exercise, mental illness and addiction are two explanations that regularly appear on the whiteboard. Are mental illness and addiction situational or dispositional attributions? The answer depends on how you think about mental illness and addiction.

Do you think about addiction as a character flaw? A weakness someone has that they just need to "get over"? Or, do you recognize the many situational factors, like life circumstances, family models, or genetic predisposition, that contribute to addiction? Similarly, with mental illness, some people tend to emphasize situational explanations, pointing to factors beyond one's control (e.g., significant trauma), whereas others point to dispositional factors (e.g., a lack of mental toughness). Research suggests that most mental illness (including addiction, which is classified as a psychological disorder by the American Psychological Association) arises from a constellation of factors. Many are well beyond a person's control (e.g., trauma, genetics), but there are also things that lie more within one's control (e.g., developing healthier thinking patterns, being in community) that can exacerbate or attenuate symptoms.

The more we can recognize the complexity of these experiences—that they are not caused by any one thing, but rather they are the result of a complex set of biological (e.g., genetics), psychological (e.g., stress), and sociocultural (e.g., attitudes about or access to mental healthcare) factors, the more accurate our understanding of others (and ourselves) will be. This richer understanding also creates space for grace. Grace to meet others where they are without judgment or hubris that we could never be in the same place, or experiencing the same thing if our own circumstances were different.

A new perspective with less emphasis on what people "deserve" also helps us to meet others with the radical generosity of Jesus. Being generous beyond what people deserve is the whole point of the parable of the workers in the vineyard in Matthew 20:1–16 where everyone receives the same amount of pay for working a different number of hours. This passage is unnerving for those of us who have spent our lives working hard, just wanting to be paid fairly. And yet, this is the heart of Jesus, to give generously. Both psychology and Jesus tell us to take the question of deserving out of the equation entirely. Instead, we should try to see people as Jesus sees them, and help them regardless of what factors we think led them to where they are. This will also require us to relinquish our illusions of control and trust in the goodness of God—the theological word for this is *providence*. Not necessarily because God's goodness protects us from hardship or injustice, but because God's goodness transcends our understanding of our current circumstances.

Psych Summary: At any given moment, the situation is a more powerful determinant of someone's behavior than their personality. Being aware that we tend to underestimate how much circumstances influence other people's actions can help us to extend more grace and understanding to our neighbors, even when they behave in ways that we find upsetting, hurtful or even, seemingly, unacceptable. We may never know the truth or understand all the circumstances that led up to a particular comment or action, but we can try to faithfully shift the balance away from blaming who they are as a person toward the complex circumstances they are navigating.

THINKING THEOLOGICALLY

> I do not understand my own actions. For I do not do what I want, but I do the very thing I hate. Now if I do what I do not want, I agree that the law is good. But in fact it is no longer I that do it, but sin that dwells within me. For I know that nothing good dwells within me, that is, in my flesh. I can will what is right, but I cannot do it. For I do not do the good I want, but the evil I do not want is what I do. Now if I do what I do not want, it is no longer I that do it, but sin that dwells within me.
>
> —Romans 7:15-20

Why do people do bad things? Is it because of who they are (their disposition) or is it because of the situation they are in? The field of social psychology acknowledges that each plays an important role, but encourages us to not underestimate the power of the situation. For Christians, the answer is similarly complicated and seems to be yes to both. Yes, people have bad behavior because of who they are (they are sinners—*but* that is not all they are). Yes, people have bad behavior because of the situations they are in (sin has affected everything). Augustine, one of the most famous church fathers from North Africa in the fourth century, explained that since "the fall" of Adam and Eve, humanity is not able to not sin; however, we were originally created very good, without sin. Our original state is our true God-given identity.

The temptation for Christians across centuries, however, is to overemphasize our sinful identity as our true or real identity. In other words, we can err on the side of claiming that being sinful is our disposition (who we really are) and not merely our situation (that state that we find ourselves in). But the book of Romans and other passages about sin and our identity seem to claim that sin is something that happens to us. In other words, sin is situational—it came into the world after the good creation existed, creating a new "you-can't-help-but-sin" situation. In Romans 7:8, Paul writes that sin "seizes an opportunity." That opportunity is to corrupt the good creation of the world.

The deeper, original truth is that we are very good, created in the image of God (Gen. 1:27), and made for loving relationships with God (1 John 4:19), ourselves (Matt. 22:37), our neighbors (Gal. 5:13–14), and the world (John 3:16). Sin and all the bad stuff that we do intentionally or unintentionally is the mark of sin in the world. A sinful world is the situation we find ourselves in.

And even here, this is not the end of the story. Second Corinthians 2:51 tells us, "He who was without sin was made to become sin for us, so that we might be the righteousness of God." For Christians, sin is a force that came into the world and changed reality.

In some ways, every person can truly say, I did this because I am a sinner. And yet, we are called to not be defined by this reality, but by the deeper and truer reality that we are born again, with a new identity that is sanctified and being made holy, because Jesus became sin for us, "so that we might be the righteousness of God."

Okay, so now that we have learned from these passages about sin and Christian identity—that Christians think sin affects everything, and yet, we are to live by the deeper truth that we were originally created good, *and* that Jesus has reconciled all things so we can live as forgiven—we can now consider what it means to take into account the situations that affect behavior, specifically how we interpret other people's bad behavior.

At a minimum, humility about our own bad behavior, or sin, should compel us to offer a gracious response to the bad behavior and suffering of others. This new knowledge from psychology can help us move toward this type of gracious response. People are sometimes in situations beyond their control that affect their behavior. They might have gotten a new, terrible diagnosis. They might have a kid who is taking their bad day out on them. They might have just had a fight with their partner. They might have just been laid off. They might be struggling with homesickness. Or they might have been abused and have carried the weight of that abuse through their entire life in silence. If we can see that the situation, and not the person, is the problem, we are more likely to respond and help with love and patience. This is true for those who are suffering publicly in society from drug addiction, who are without homes, or who are employed in sex work, but it also applies to small daily interactions.

Imagine that your boss forgot to add your overtime hours, your roommate left the sink full of dirty dishes, you got a terrible night of sleep, or the kid in your life is melting down about McDonald's putting ketchup on their plain hamburger. Situations like these do not bring out the best in us. Noticing that these situations are frustrating and make it difficult to show up in ways we feel good about can help us interpret our own actions more generously as well. We can recognize that we are good people in a tough situation. We are good and loved. We are also redeemed and forgiven. Recognizing our sin and accepting forgiveness presents us with the freedom to live into this beautiful, bold reality.

Further, recognizing that all of humanity is in need of forgiveness for sin that only Jesus can offer puts us on equal standing with everyone else. The reformed theologian John Calvin wrote that when we recognize and understand the significance of this, our response is to live lives marked by grace toward others and gratitude toward God.

LIVING FAITHFULLY

Consider something you've done that you know was wrong: Did you do it because you are a bad person or because of bad circumstances? How might you interact with people differently if you were to think first, "They are a good person in a tough situation." Most of us would readily forgive someone who, like Aladdin in the Disney classic, stole bread because he was poor and hungry. Aladdin is not merely a *thief*, but a person who stole something because he was hungry and poor. An initial principle like "It is not okay to steal" might soften when we understand the circumstance. This wider-lens understanding would likely change how we treat the person. We would likely be more compassionate when talking with Aladdin about his choices, and perhaps even try to help address the situation he was in (without enough money to buy food). Put simply, seeing the circumstance can create space for deeper and more merciful interactions.

Let's consider another example, an attempt at murder. For most people this action feels so extreme that jumping to a dispositional explanation, that only the most horrible and vile of people could ever do something like that, feels easily justifiable. We are willing to bet, however, that there are situations or circumstances that could at least complicate, if not entirely change, your assessment of the attempted murderer's character.

For example, what if the target of the attempted murder was Adolf Hitler at the height of his reign in Nazi Germany? Seems more complicated now, doesn't it?

We know this example probably seems outlandish, but it isn't fiction. This was the moral dilemma that Dietrich Bonhoeffer, a well-known Lutheran pastor and theologian, found himself in. Bonhoeffer lived in Germany in the 1930s. His credentials made it possible for him to take refuge in America during this tumultuous time and he did so, twice. During his second visit, he wrote, "I have come to the conclusion that I made a mistake in coming to America. I must live through this difficult period in our national history with the people of Germany. I will have no right to participate in the reconstruction of Christian life in Germany after the war if I do not share the trials of this time with my people."[4]

Throughout his life Bonhoeffer was critical of Christians who claimed that a pious faith, without living out their beliefs, was enough. Holding himself to the same standard, he returned to Germany, with a deep sense of calling to do what he could to protect oppressed groups in Germany. Upon his return, Bonhoeffer had the opportunity to be involved in an assassination attempt on Hitler. A suitcase bomb was planted near Hitler's desk. The bomb failed to kill Hitler, and there are speculations that the failure can be chalked up to the hefty wooden desk that bore the brunt of the explosion. Bonhoeffer was eventually arrested and killed in a concentration camp for his involvement.

Theologians still debate about whether Bonhoeffer should have gone through with the assassination attempt, and according to all accounts, it appears Bonhoeffer was also deeply morally conflicted about the decision. Whether it was the right or the wrong decision is ultimately not ours to judge, and certainly a conversation for another time (if you are desperate to have this conversation, perhaps you belong in seminary!). The point here is that the situation matters *a lot*.

Knowing that the person attempting murder was a Christian leader in Germany during the Third Reich *and* that the person they were trying to murder was Hitler changes the way we think about the would-be assassin. If we would have just written this would-be murderer off as a terrible person, we would be dismissing a revolutionary theologian who wrote vulnerably about his complicated struggle to live out his faith, not merely to talk about it, during a genocide.

All of us make judgments about people's characters when we do not have the full story. Our perception of something as rude, unacceptable, or even morally repugnant when we view it as an isolated action might change if we take a more holistic perspective that incorporates the circumstances. The goal is not to excuse harmful behaviors but to continue to hold onto the image of God's goodness inside every person, even when their actions initially seem inexcusable. Giving others the benefit of the doubt and seeking more information to understand the circumstances or situation more completely may give you a very different perspective.

Reconsider the action you identified at the very beginning of this chapter, a time when someone hurt you. Instead of a dispositional attribution, what situational attributions could you make instead? If that story or situation is too painful for you to unpack now, think of something less hurtful, perhaps a rude classmate, being cut off in traffic, or someone talking loudly on their phone on a bus.

SITUATIONAL ATTRIBUTIONS:

1.

2.

3.

What if that rude classmate had a migraine, the person cutting you off in traffic was racing to the hospital with a woman in labor, and the person talking loudly on the bus was checking in on his grandmother who lives alone? Notice how these situational attributions change the way you feel about the person and the scenario. As you listed the situational attributions that might explain the behavior in your scenario, did you feel your annoyance or anger lessen?

Situational attributions may not excuse the behavior entirely or change the hurt it caused, but they can potentially help us move, even a little bit, toward a place of understanding and forgiveness. In much the same way that God views us, not as bad people but as children whom he loves unconditionally who are afflicted by sinful circumstances, let us love those around us with a heart to see their true identity as good people created in the image of God.

six

RECOGNIZING EVERYONE'S FULL HUMANITY

The poor are disliked even by their neighbors,
but the rich have many friends.

—Proverbs 14:20

LEARNING FROM PSYCHOLOGY

As Christians, we believe that all people are created in God's image. This does not mean that we are all exactly the same; each human is unique. It does, however, mean that we all carry the same value, worth, and dignity because of who we are and whose we are. God loves each of us immeasurably more than we can comprehend. Perhaps in an effort to formalize these values, the writers of the Declaration of Independence included the phrase "all men are created equal." And yet we know that women and people of color were not automatically granted equal opportunities. Black women, for example, were not allowed to vote until 1965 (more than 180 years after the Declaration of Independence was written). It wasn't until 1974 that a woman could open a bank account without a male cosigner and that all people were protected from credit discrimination based on race.[1] The history of the United States is, and continues to be, stained with examples and policies that very clearly place a higher value on some people than others—the history of enslavement and forced racial segregation in the United States are other examples. From a theological perspective, these policies reveal a failure to honor the *imago Dei* in every person. They also reveal something that social psychologists are constantly measuring—specifically, negative attitudes toward groups of people with whom we do not identify.

There are many ways to measure such attitudes. Arguably one of the most influential and enduring is the *stereotype content model*, which suggests we make judgments about other groups of people based on two key questions.[2]

1. On average, how warm (friendly) are people from this group?
2. On average, how competent are people from this group?

Let's practice for a second. Below is a set of four quadrants you could use to map people. The fire and ice icons represent the warmth dimension. The small brain and big brain represent the competence dimension. Warm and competent groups would, thus, be located in the top right quadrant, whereas cold and incompetent groups would be located in the bottom left.

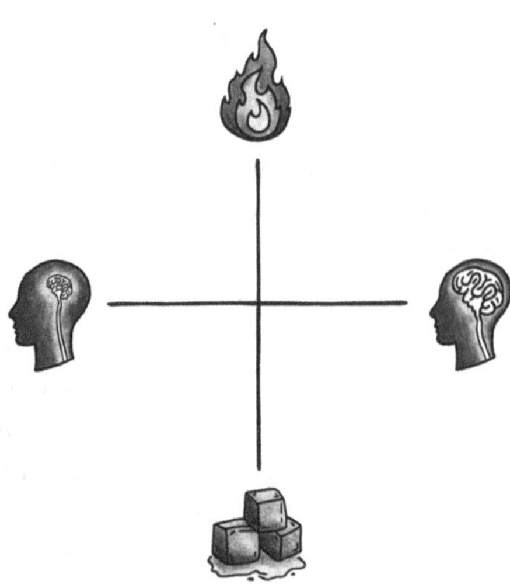

Consider the following groups and place them somewhere along the continuum. You can simply tap your finger somewhere on the diagram, or you can write the numbers for each group (1–10) somewhere within the four quadrants.

1. People experiencing homelessness
2. Refugees
3. Lawyers
4. Grandmothers
5. Immigrants
6. Babies
7. Muslims
8. Democrats
9. Republicans
10. Pet owners

The lower in warmth or competence any group is perceived (the closer you place them to the bottom left), the more negative our perceptions of them and the more likely our response to that group will be either contempt (thinking that we are better than them) or apathy (not thinking about them at all). But how do we go from looking down on someone or not caring about them to actively harming them? Many argue that an even more extreme negative attitude about others, that they are less human than we are, may help to explain the most atrocious forms of violence. At face value, this may seem odd. Of course, we know all humans are . . . fully human. But that does not mean that we believe all humans fully embody the complexities of what it means to be human.

From a psychological perspective, dehumanization is systematically thinking of other people as having fewer human-like traits, needs, or abilities than you have. For example, any time you think someone has less self-control, seems less capable of experiencing complex emotions like shame or guilt, or cares less about high-level needs like experiencing purpose in their work and life than you, you are engaging in a subtle form of dehumanizing that person. These assessments (whether correct or incorrect) will impact how you treat that person. When similar perceptions are extended to an entire group of people, the consequences will reach far beyond one-on-one interactions.

Because psychologists tend to measure dehumanization based on perceptions of *groups* rather than asking about *individuals*, these findings reveal something even more insidious than discriminating against or denying God's image in a single person. We aren't simply saying one particular person has less ability or value (as problematic as that is). We are systematically underestimating, undervaluing, or dehumanizing entire groups of people. Take in what that means. These studies show over and over again that people consistently report that entire groups of people (often the groups they identify with the least) have fewer abilities than other groups of people. We are also quick to report that our own groups are more refined, more warm, more capable, more evolved than other groups to which we do not belong.

The belief that some people are worse, less capable, less valuable or otherwise "less than" simply because of a group to which they belong is the root of racism, sexism, and ableism (to name but a few). The belief that Jewish people were inferior was at the core of what fueled the genocide of Jews during World War II. The belief that Black people were an inferior race led to slavery and the detainment of people of color in the United States and around the world. Beliefs that rank groups as better and worse continue to fuel atrocities. Ranking the value of people is in direct contradiction to the Christian belief that God created each individual with dignity, and that their worth does not come from comparisons between or the perceptions of others.

If we really believe God created us all equally, entire groups should not have (or be perceived to have) more or less of these human-like traits and abilities than any other group (we are talking about averages here). And if there actually are differences, on average, in groups, then we have to ask ourselves the really hard question, What is causing these differences? We know God didn't create some people groups who are better or more capable of certain forms of success or kindness than others, so there must be another explanation.

Have you ever caught yourself saying or thinking, "If ____ (people) just worked harder, exerted more self-control, or took more pride in their work, then they wouldn't _____"? These statements assume group-level differences, that an entire group is lacking in traits or abilities. Blanket judgments like these are especially problematic for groups who have been historically marginalized or oppressed because they place blame on the individuals in the group rather than looking at the external factors that might be causing real or perceived differences. One way of thinking about this is to compare how we assign praise and blame to wealth and poverty. Do we praise a rich person who comes from a rich family for their inherited wealth (what incredible work ethic!) as much as we blame a poor person, raised in a poor family, for their inherited poverty (if only they had some work ethic!)? We suspect not. We can see inherited wealth for what it is, something beyond the person's doing, but we struggle to see inherited poverty in the same way.

Let's go back to the topic of homelessness. Here is a common blanket judgment: If homeless individuals just worked harder, then they wouldn't be homeless. If we really believe we were all created equal and in the image of God, then we have to ask ourselves, Are there any circumstances I could learn about individuals experiencing homelessness that would change my interpretation of them? What if I learned that most individuals experiencing homelessness had experienced a traumatic event in their lives, or grew up in poverty, or were afflicted by chronic illnesses, or had parents with mental illnesses? Common situational factors are far more likely to drive group-level differences than common dispositional factors. There is no scientific evidence that one group of people, from a different country or racial identity, is less capable, hardworking, or intelligent than another. And yet, even with this knowledge and the conviction that all people deserve to be treated with dignity, we are prone to stereotype and dehumanize other people.

One important step in disrupting our tendency to dehumanize others is being open to the possibility that situations matter, as do context and history. The benefits of hearing others' stories and learning more about their situations can also help us to see and recognize the common humanity we share. Curiosity about another person's circumstances is sometimes all it takes to enhance our capacity for a deeper and more Christ-like compassion.

Because dehumanization is consequential for how we treat people, it is worth learning about the nuances of dehumanizing perspectives and what can be done to reduce them. Dehumanization is often thought to take one of two forms depending on the types of traits or needs you deny to someone else. *Animalistic dehumanization* is the result of underestimating the complex cognitive abilities of others—like self-control or a need for meaning in life—or thinking of them as less evolved (e.g., like an ape). In essence, we liken people to nonhuman animals. One of the clearest examples of this is in the language we use to describe groups. At the most extreme ends, we directly refer to others in animalistic terms. The Declaration of Independence provides another poignant example of this very form of animalistic dehumanization. When citing a list of evidence against the king of Britain to justify secession, the declaration reads,

> He [the king of Great Britain] has excited domestic insurrections amongst us, and has endeavoured to bring on the inhabitants of our frontiers, the merciless Indian Savages, whose known rule of warfare, is an undistinguished destruction of all ages, sexes and conditions.

Referring to Native Americans as "merciless savages" who have an "undistinguished" form of warfare are two ways that animalistic dehumanization is blatantly documented in the legal foundations of the United States. Unfortunately, examples abound throughout history highlighting how such derogatory and sometimes directly animalistic language (calling people monkeys, pigs, rats, or dogs) often accompanies acts of violence and aggression toward the targeted group. Recently, the language of "infestation" was used to refer to people who were trying to migrate to the United States. This language is insidious because the more we talk about a people group in animalistic terms, the less we identify with them (as fellow humans) and the easier it is to treat them merely as unwelcome animals to be contained, caged, or controlled rather than God's children to be seen, heard, cared for, and loved.

The other form of dehumanization is referred to as *mechanistic dehumanization*. Here, there is an acknowledgment of others' competence, but an underestimation of their depth, warmth, or ability to experience complex emotions. It is almost like they are perceived as highly capable robots without feelings or cultural complexity. The people we dehumanize in this way may be useful to us because they are capable and intelligent, but we are unlikely to care deeply for people whom we dehumanize in this way. At the group level, mechanistic dehumanization may not be as directly connected to active harm, but it is connected with a lack of deep concern or care. In essence, this form of dehumanization leads to seeing people as tools or means to an end, not "worthy" of our time or mental and emotional energies.

Dehumanization matters, not only because it is antithetical to the way we are called to acknowledge the *imago Dei* in others, but also because it is directly connected to the ways that we fail to love others. This may be subtle, what psychologists refer to as *passive harm*, when we forgo an opportunity to help or advocate for those in need, or more extreme acts, what psychologists refer to as *active harm*, when we act in ways that directly thwart the health and well-being of others. The research is clear: maintaining dehumanizing attitudes toward others is never going to help us love them better.

So, how do we disrupt dehumanization?

One of the most powerful ways to change attitudes is through contact with those whom we dehumanize. This means having meaningful interpersonal interactions. Gordon Allport's *contact hypothesis* suggests that contact needs to meet several criteria to be effective at reducing dehumanization or negative attitudes about out-group members (people who belong to a group that we don't identify with).[3] These include the following:

1. Interdependence: When interactions require us to rely on one another (we can't do it alone), they promote humanizing attitudes.
2. Common Goal: When interactions require people to work together toward a common goal, they promote humanizing attitudes.
3. Equal Status: When interactions are between two people of equal status (no power dynamics or differentials) and make space for what everyone can offer, they promote humanizing attitudes.
4. Neutral Setting: When interactions take place in a casual and neutral location that feels safe and friendly to both people (rather than on one person's "home turf"), they promote humanizing attitudes.
5. Multiple Interactions: When interactions include multiple members, not just one person, from a dehumanized group, they promote humanizing attitudes.
6. Socially Valued: When interactions are supported and recognized as valuable within a particular context (e.g., a family, a company, a city), they promote humanizing attitudes.

Let us be honest. That is a long and complicated list! And most interactions we have with those we dehumanize do not even tick a few (let alone all) of those boxes. When was the last time you sat down in a friendly environment with someone experiencing homelessness to have a chat with the shared goal of simply enjoying your time together? In other words, you did not maintain a position of power and abundance by "handing out" the food to others in need, but let yourself experience fellowship with them.[4] Our guess is that most of us have honestly never had this type of interaction with even one person from the people groups we dehumanize the most, let alone multiple people from that group! But how much richer would our understanding of others be and, thus, our ability to love them well if we were intentional about these types of interactions.

To answer that question, we had our own students share (not serve) a meal with individuals experiencing homelessness in hopes of helping them recognize their shared humanity.[5]

To pull this off in a rigorous and scientific way, we needed to have some students have a shared interaction that met as many of the six criteria of the contact hypothesis as possible and then compare their attitudes to other students who did not have a shared meal interaction. Luckily, we teach a lot of classes. So, we randomly assigned three classes of Introductory Theology students to a shared meal assignment. The students in these classes attended one free community dinner, not as volunteers to serve but simply to enjoy a meal with whoever else might be at the table. The assignment was to meet a neighbor that you do not yet know and write a short reflection paper about your experience.[6] The other three classes of Introductory Theology students completed their course as usual, without having the dinner assignment.

Did the shared meal experience work to reduce dehumanization?

Well, it depends on how you define *work*. The experience of table fellowship our students had was a rich one that allowed them to see and name many uniquely human traits and abilities of another person who is currently unhoused. In this way, the interaction created space for a more humanizing interaction. Was it enough to disrupt dehumanizing stereotypes of people experiencing homelessness as a whole? No. Our findings suggest that the recognition of someone's humanity was limited to the particular individual with whom the students shared a meal, but it did not change the way they thought of individuals experiencing homelessness as a whole. (Likely because we were missing criterion number five from Allport's contact hypothesis—multiple interactions with people from the other group.)

Was it valuable? Yes, because dehumanizing attitudes, like stereotypes, can be changed one person at a time. Notice the contact hypothesis requires interactions with multiple group members. The more interactions our students have with people experiencing homelessness, the more likely they will shed their dehumanizing stereotypes and replace them with humanizing interpretations.

Having a one-off interaction that counters stereotypes does not change stereotypes. Why? Because in just one interaction (or multiple interactions with the same person) we see that person as an exception, rather than an exemplar of the group. Whether it is conscious or not, we mentally separate the person from their group rather than seeing them as a clear representation of the entire group. This is why it is possible to have a good friend (or even a few) who belongs to a group that you otherwise hold negative attitudes about or dehumanize on the whole. You do not use your friend to update your impressions of the entire group; you mentally distance them from the group seeing them as an exception unlike "most" people in that group.

Another way to disrupt dehumanization is to be aware of how it is likely to shape the way you treat others. One way we dehumanize others is when we assume they have fewer higher-level needs than we do. For example, we might assume that leading a purposeful and meaningful life is less important to them. If we make this assumption, we are less likely to try to help them reach their higher-level goals like pursuing a career or offering them résumé support. Instead, we will focus on lower-level physical needs like providing a free meal.

Nicholas Epley and Juliana Schroeder demonstrated how these misperceptions can result in a disconnect between the type of help we think others need and the type of help others want for themselves. Nearly 76 percent of college students endorsed a meal program, rather than a wellness program, for individuals who are unhoused. However, when those who were unhoused were asked what program they wanted, the minority—approximately 48 percent—chose the meal program. The remaining 52 percent of individuals experiencing homelessness chose the wellness program for themselves.[7]

These findings suggest a drastic mismatch between the type of help we think people need and that type of help they actually want. This mismatch is driven, in large part, by a failure to appreciate the complexity and richness of others whom we tend to dehumanize the most.

While there is nothing wrong with offering physical support (and of course it is needed!), it should not be the only type of support we offer.

Psych Summary: The dehumanizing attitudes we hold about others are not always obvious, but they do impact our ability to love others well. Recognizing when you have thoughts that insist other people or groups have "less" of a cognitive or emotional trait or ability than you do can help you to be more aware of how you might be accidentally denying other people their full humanity.

To fight dehumanization, you can engage in equal-status interactions. Not the types of interactions where you sit comfortably in a position of power (like a boss with an employee) or a place of abundance (like a volunteer passing out food at a homeless shelter), but the messy types of interactions where two people depend on one another, even if only in the sense that you need each other to be present and engage equally to have a meaningful conversation or shared experience. Engaging in this way might just help you appreciate the nuances and needs that make us all human.

THINKING THEOLOGICALLY

> Wealth brings many friends,
> but the poor are left friendless. . . .
> If the poor are hated even by their kin,
> how much more are they shunned by their friends!
> When they call after them, they are not there.
>
> —Proverbs 19:4, 7

> The poor are disliked even by their neighbors,
> but the rich have many friends.
> Those who despise their neighbors are sinners,
> but happy are those who are kind to the poor. . . .
> Those who oppress the poor insult their Maker,
> but those who are kind to the needy honor him.
>
> —Proverbs 14:20–21, 31

The wisdom literature in the Bible has a lot to say about fairness, poverty, and human dignity. A quick skim of Proverbs reveals how people tend to favor and show preference toward the rich (they have more friends!) than the poor, who are hated even by their kin, or family. Proverbs ties our treatment of those who are poor to the ways we insult or honor God. To treat those who are poor with kindness and dignity is to honor God. Those who oppress others insult God. Unfortunately, we are often blind to the ways we oppress others, until we are confronted by our own hypocrisy.

Here is a glorious example of one of our own confrontations with hypocrisy in this realm.

> "It's the most amazing place," I told my friend as we walked a few blocks from my home to the Aurora Commons. The Aurora Commons was created in 2008 when friends from the Awake Church took seriously the call to love their neighbor. Sparrow Etter Carlson, Karen Sullivan (Cirulli), and Ben Katt walked the track along Aurora

Avenue, one of two tracks where women in sex work are picked up in Seattle, talking to women, meeting the front desk attendants of the hotels and motels along Aurora, and prayerfully wondering how to love these specific neighbors engaged in sex work.

After hundreds of conversations in the neighborhood and many backyard barbecues for these and any neighbors who were drawn to the delicious smells, they felt called, along with their congregation, to rent some space and create a "neighborhood living room." At this church, their money for a building goes to this shared vision dubbed the "Aurora Commons," not a Sunday morning worship space. For worship, the church meets in a Chinese restaurant called Jade next to the Commons.

The interior of the Commons is beautiful, with a full kitchen, a fireplace, a long dining room table that seats at least twenty, comfortable couches, shelves of books, a couple of showers, and a washer and dryer. It has a hipster vibe with live edge wood, a collection of thrifted chandeliers hanging from the ceiling, and a piano, whose keys do not collect dust. Not only are they helping people but the place looks really cool, and I feel awesome (and pretty cool) supporting this ministry. This "neighborhood living room" is in my neighborhood, literally four blocks from my house. Those who gather there are my neighbors.

This particular evening the Aurora Commons was hosting a community art gallery, all the art having been created by people in the neighborhood. I had contributed a painting that would hang on the wall alongside the art of my neighbors. This art was made by those who live in houses or apartments as well as those who live in hotels, cars, and tents. There was art by those who engage in sex as paid work as well as those who do not engage in sex as paid work. There was supposed to be an open mic for poetry and my artsy White lady heart was bursting with excitement to support such a noble cause through my presence, in addition to my regular financial donations.

We walked in to find a lovely charcuterie plate with cheese, crackers, and grapes, as well as wine for all in attendance. I don't

> think I was quite able to hide the raise of my eyebrows as I thought, "They are serving wine to prostitutes?!" Didn't they want to help people? Don't they know how the Methodists started the trend to serve grape juice instead of wine at church to keep alcoholics from stumbling? But I am Presbyterian, so I managed to lower my eyebrows and walked over to the snacks, casually pouring myself a glass of wine.
>
> My friend and I walked through the space meeting people and making small talk, and I have to admit that I was again unsettled because I could not tell who was a sex worker and who was just a normal "not-sex-worker" person from the neighborhood. I suddenly felt hot and sweaty and nervous with the horrible thought, "Oh my gosh, what if someone thinks I am a prostitute?" I could honestly not tell the difference, and I bet other people couldn't either. I knew one guy who was the pastor of the congregation that helped birth the Aurora Commons and I recognized a few other faces, but as I looked around I honestly couldn't tell who was who. How could I signal that I was just a *regular* person from the neighborhood? Somehow the Aurora Commons had created a space where everyone was just a human person. Everyone was able to just talk to each other, without titles or labels creating a social hierarchy, and it was completely disorienting. The rich and the poor were friends.

It is honestly a bit embarrassing to share this story, but it exposes the dynamics that can mark our genuine desire to love someone while simultaneously not wanting to be associated with them, or (God forbid) mistaken for "one of them." Perhaps you have had a similar moment of mistaken identity. "Oh no" (insert coy chuckle), you might have responded to someone assuming you were a client rather than a volunteer at the food pantry, "I'm not here to *pick up* food, I am here to *hand it out*." The subtext to this is "I am not one of the ones who need help, I am a helper. I am self-sufficient and independent." When we make these distinctions, we reinforce dehumanizing stereotypes, presenting ourselves as more likable, one of the rich who have "many friends" rather than the "poor [who] are left friendless" (Prov. 19:4).

Part of what is so incredible about the Aurora Commons is that these are people who are friends with women engaged in sex work, just like Jesus was. They are the most Christ-like people I know. And if I am honest, I don't have a single friend who is a prostitute. Not one. And clearly, I would be horrified if my profession was assumed to be a sex worker. Experiences like these are memorable and potentially transformative because they put into stark relief the challenge of loving our literal neighbors, whom we are more comfortable ignoring and avoiding because being near them is socially awkward. I genuinely believe that every person bears the image of God, has dignity, and deserves to be treated in humanizing ways, but I find it extremely difficult to interact in ways that are different from the ways I have been socialized to interact with specific groups. Moments like these remind me of my own hypocritical and imperfectly human attempts to live out my faith.

Theologically what is at stake is human dignity. Christians believe that each person is created by God, bears the image of God, is loved by God, and is the dwelling place of God. Because of this, each person deserves to be treated with dignity and love, as though they are competent and warm, to use the psychological terms. First Corinthians 3:16 says, "Do you not know that you are God's temple, and that God's Spirit dwells in you?" Each person bears the image of God (Gen. 1:27), bears the likeness of Christ, and is the temple of the Spirit. Yet, we often try to distance ourselves from others, reinforce differences, and maintain boundaries that are ultimately dehumanizing to the "other."

This is not faithful and it is an insult to God. Replace "rich" and "poor" in the passages in Proverbs with "housed" and "unhoused" or "citizen" and "refugee" or "non-sex worker" and "sex worker," and you can see how socially preferable some identities are to others, and these distinctions lead us to dehumanize others. What is so profound about the ministry of the Aurora Commons is that in all areas of their ministry they disrupt social hierarchies, inviting neighbors to come together, not so that one group can serve another but to eat bread and drink wine with a merry heart (Eccles. 9:7) while celebrating the creativity present in our shared neighborhood.

LIVING FAITHFULLY

In our research we learned that the types of interactions we have with people matter significantly for how we view them. Some interactions help us see ourselves as equally human while other types of interactions can promote the tendency to see others as less than human. Christians are often comfortable serving, being the helper, or the giver, but often less comfortable being served, receiving help, or accepting a gift. Unfortunately, if we are only ever giving or serving, we can fall prey to the dehumanizing belief that we are better than those we serve. One way to disrupt this is to spend time in different roles that we are not used to.

During COVID, those living in Seattle were able to pick up groceries and free lunches at the local elementary school. This social program was set up to employ those looking for jobs, provide food for families in the neighborhood (regardless of their income), and provide a connection to the school for kids who were missing in-person classes. Many people in the neighborhood came together to utilize this resource, regardless of their financial status, because it created a space for community and supported underemployed neighbors. It also helped kids stay connected to their school in a way that they might not have otherwise.

When we reframe the distribution of physical resources (like free groceries, clothes, or dinners) as gathering places where community and care can happen, we begin to see that participation isn't only about physical needs, but also middle-level (e.g., belonging) and high-level (e.g., purpose) needs. Our participation in these spaces allows us not only to contribute to community but also to be blessed by community.

- In what ways might you consider stepping into a "role reversal" where you show up as a member of a community, rather than as someone who has something (time, knowledge, resources) to give others? Consider leaning into one of these ideas: If your neighborhood has a free community dinner, you might plan to attend as a guest (not a host or volunteer) and meet someone. Rather than serving a meal, which reinforces the idea that "you need food and I need purpose, which is why I volunteer," sit down and share a meal together. You might pretend you are one of our students and start your meal together by asking, "I am new to this dinner, do you mind if I sit with you?" Then you might ask, "What is your story?" or "How long have you lived in this area? What creative passions or hobbies do you have? Would you tell me a story about someone who makes you smile?"
- We can also take time to acknowledge ways we can give (and experience) beyond the low-level human needs like food and shelter. How might we invest in people by helping them acquire job skills, share their creativity, or discern what wellness might look like for them at this stage of life? Perhaps your business could be intentional about hiring a few people a year who are coming out of the prison system instead of just donating money, or you could volunteer at your local library to help people edit their résumés or apply for internships. Like the Aurora Commons, you might make sure the space where people receive support is beautiful, somewhere you would also want to spend time. These types of interactions will be more uncomfortable because our society is set up to keep us in a hierarchy, but you can choose to disrupt this, and in doing so, treat people as humans who have meaningful lives to live in your neighborhood.
- If you are in a situation where you can offer help, the way you do it matters. One simple and humanizing shift you can make is to ask people what they need rather than making assumptions about what they need. This small change allows us to

love others the way they want and need to be loved rather than how it is easiest or most comfortable for us to love them. This might be as simple as asking someone if they are hungry and if so, what their food preferences are (rather than assuming they'd want your half-eaten leftovers). It could also mean giving a gift card instead of an item to honor someone's autonomy and human need to make decisions for themselves.

seven

LETTING GO OF CONTEMPT

Let no evil talk come out of your mouths.

—Ephesians 4:29

LEARNING FROM PSYCHOLOGY

According to Elie Wiesel, a gifted writer, professor, and Nobel laureate, "The opposite of love is not hate, it is indifference."[1] And indeed, we have seen that failing to care about or notice other people gets in the way of neighbor love.

Curiously, however, a defining aspect of Elie Wiesel's life was not characterized by indifference at all, but rather being on the receiving end of direct, intentional, and deep-seated hatred. Wiesel was Jewish and lived in Hungary during the German occupation in 1944. He, his father, sister, and mother were all imprisoned in Auschwitz, one of the most well-known concentration camps. His sister and mother were killed there. Wiesel and his father were eventually taken to a second concentration camp. Wiesel, still a teenager when the camp was liberated in 1945, was the only family member to survive.

The manifestation of this hatred was not simply passive harm but rather *active harm*. Undoubtedly the mass genocide of Jews and others Hitler deemed "unworthy" during World War II depicts the most explicit and horrific forms of active harm. The committee who awarded Wiesel the Nobel Prize spoke of Hitler's *contempt* for humanity, the hate that made these atrocities possible. Psychological research supports the strong connection between contempt and active harm toward others. Importantly, however, contempt is not an emotion exclusive to those who perpetrate unthinkable evil. We all feel and express contempt toward others at times, and the consequences are insidious.

So, what exactly is *contempt*? According to psychologists, when someone feels contempt for another person, they look down on them, thinking of themselves as morally (or otherwise) superior. Disgust, one of the most common emotions tied to contempt, is often directed at the same groups who are viewed with contempt. Disgust is a natural emotion and is useful in some contexts (helping us to avoid potential harm from illness or disease when something smells foul or turn away from horrific acts of violence, for example). When directed at a particular person (or group of people), however, it tends to distance them from the image of God in our minds and lead us away from, rather than toward, a loving and humanizing response.

As we have already discussed, individuals experiencing homelessness are one of the most widely stereotyped and highly dehumanized groups. They are regularly placed in the lower left quadrant on the warmth and competence scale that you learned about in the previous chapter. Viewing pictures of individuals experiencing homelessness also activates brain areas that are associated with feelings of disgust. These feelings tend to manifest in physically distancing ourselves from those we perceive with contempt. Brittany's research has shown a strong association between dehumanizing attitudes and behaviors. The greater the dehumanization, the more likely people are to actively distance themselves (socially and physically) from individuals experiencing homelessness by avoiding eye contact or crossing over to the other side of the street. Interestingly, the link between attitudes and actions was strongest for individuals who reported that social justice was of low importance to them. For individuals reporting high social justice importance, there was not a strong link between dehumanization and avoidance. In essence, caring about social justice helped prevent any dehumanizing attitudes from translating into dehumanizing behavior.[2] Contempt and a lack of care or concern for social justice issues are incongruent with the type of contact required to improve perceptions of others.

Contempt is consistently linked to particular groups of people whom we dehumanize. This can be seen in our perceptions of those experiencing homelessness, but we can also experience contempt (in waves or consistently) for a single person. There may be moments in your relationships when you treat others with contempt, or you demean them. If you have ever found yourself mocking your partner or using a belittling tone in an argument, you have been guilty of treating those in your life with contempt. Trust us: you are not alone.

It might be easy to brush these moments of sarcasm and eyerolls aside or not take them seriously, but psychological research, largely pioneered by John Gottman, suggests that even these seemingly small displays of contempt toward our partners are some of the best predictors of divorce.[3] Beyond predicting the health of your romantic relationship, contemptuous behaviors also predict how likely it is that your partner will experience certain physical health issues!

Being on the receiving end of contempt is linked to physical and psychological damage. Why? One proposed explanation is that these displays of contempt are perceived as signals that our lives, needs, or ideas do not have value. We don't know about you, but for us, the reality of this research hits home a little too hard. When we think about times we have acted in contemptuous ways, it is often people we love and care about the most who have been on the receiving end. Perhaps it is because feelings of contempt toward people (or groups) we are not in direct contact with do not have as great an opportunity to manifest into any sort of tangible behavior. But when we think about our kids, our relatives, our colleagues, or our spouses, it is easy to see how an air of moral superiority sneaks into our daily interactions.

Clearly contempt impedes our ability to love our neighbors (including our close friends and family) well, not only because we are unlikely to help them but because experiencing contempt and dehumanization can actually change the way people think about themselves. Research exploring the consequences of being on the receiving end of contempt and dehumanization has shown these negative impacts. In particular, being perceived as less human by others can actually reduce the extent to which people think about themselves as fully human. Additionally, being on the receiving end of dehumanization or contempt can instigate retaliation and a willingness to harm an out-group. In other words, when we dehumanize others or treat them with contempt, we increase the likelihood that they will begin to dehumanize themselves and also that they will act with animosity toward us. This is clearly not a recipe for neighbor love nor a path by which we can readily appreciate that we all bear the image of God.

Thankfully, John Gottman has also spent time researching solutions for countering contempt in relationships. First and foremost, it is important to be aware of contemptuous behavior. It may not feel like you are treating others with contempt on purpose (and we believe that is true!), but the research is not about intentions; it is about actions. The actions are problematic no matter what the intention, so those are what we need to focus on eliminating. Examples range from sarcasm and eye-rolling to mockery and hostile humor.

While it might be easy to hide behind these behaviors as small meaningless gestures, they are far from harmless. The primary antidote to contempt is being intentional about creating a culture of respect and appreciation. This means that the jokes we tell, the way we talk to our friends about our partners and kids even when they aren't around, all should honor and respect that person (or people group's) full humanity. One thing we have been working on lately is trying to remind ourselves (because we do believe it) that everyone has something to teach us—that there is something we can learn from every person we encounter and every interaction we have. Approaching our interactions with curiosity and a desire to learn from others can help to eliminate opportunities for the lie that we are "better" than anyone else to creep in and embolden our contemptuous behaviors.

The other primary suggestion for countering contempt in our relationships is to express your gratitude and appreciation for others, a lot. Like, way more than you think you need to. Gottman's work suggests a "golden ratio" of five to one.[4] The healthiest marriages, the ones that go the distance, are the marriages where the positive interactions far outweigh the negatives. If you say or do something hurtful, it is going to take, on average, five genuine positive exchanges of a similar magnitude to begin to counter that hurt. A one-to-one ratio of positive to negative is not even close to enough. So before you roll your eyes or use that voice (you know the one) you use to mock your partner, think about how they will perceive those verbal and nonverbal messages. To your partner these messages scream, "Your thoughts and ideas have no value." How long will it take before they stop sharing them with you at all?

Psych Summary: Contempt is an emotion characterized by a sense of personal, and often moral, superiority relative to another person. It is commonly associated with feelings of disgust for the other person or group. Contempt toward others predicts how likely you are to harm them. It is also damaging for the health of people and relationships. Countering contempt requires effort to cultivate a culture of respect and appreciation that far outweighs (five to one) negative interactions, especially those that demean or devalue another person.

THINKING THEOLOGICALLY

> Let no evil talk come out of your mouths, but only what is useful for building up, as there is need, so that your words may give grace to those who hear. And do not grieve the Holy Spirit of God, with which you were marked with a seal for the day of redemption. Put away from you all bitterness and wrath and anger and wrangling and slander, together with all malice, and be kind to one another, tenderhearted, forgiving one another, as God in Christ has forgiven you.
>
> —Ephesians 4:29–32

Paul's letter to the people living in Ephesus is all about how their lives, their gentile lives, will be different now that they have been baptized into the body of Jesus Christ. Ephesians is one of the shorter books of the Bible, and if you have the time, we encourage you to go read it as a letter written to you. Ephesians has beautiful lines like, "so that, with the eyes of your heart enlightened, you may know what is the hope to which he has called you" (Eph. 1:18). He tells them how they all (Paul included) were "children of wrath" (Eph. 2:3), but now, because of God's gift of love, they are saved and made for good (Eph. 2:4–10).

There are likely moments when all of us can identify with being "children of wrath." There are moments when we think cruel, mean things, times when in our rage we wish terrible, unspeakable things on others, even those we love the most. We all have dark moments when something awful happens to another person and we think, "You deserved that." Or, someone disagrees with us and we silently (or perhaps loudly and with vigor) retort, "You couldn't possibly understand; you're not as _____ [insert your own adjective of inflated superiority here] as me." As noted above, when we treat others with contempt, when we are cruel to others, when we despise them, when we look down on them as if they are less than us, it actually harms them. The saying "Sticks and stones may break my bones, but words will never hurt me" is false. Words do hurt, not only on the surface; they hurt how people think about themselves. When people begin to think less of themselves, they will likely respond in kind. When we act with disgust and contempt, we are contributing to a spiral of hate, cruelty, and death. Life in Christ is supposed to be marked by exactly the opposite, a spiral of love, kindness, and life.

Paul is really concerned about how people treat each other, and so this theme appears in more than one of his letters. In his letter to the people living in Rome, Paul writes,

> Why do you pass judgment on your brother or sister? Or you, why do you despise your brother or sister? For we will all stand before the judgment seat of God. For it is written,
>
> > "As I live, says the Lord, every knee shall bow to me,
> > and every tongue shall give praise to God."
>
> So then, each of us will be accountable to God.
>
> Let us therefore no longer pass judgment on one another, but resolve instead never to put a stumbling block or hindrance in the way of another.
>
> —Romans 14:10–13

It is a natural human tendency to make judgments about other people. Within milliseconds of seeing or meeting someone, we nonconsciously size them up on a number of psychological dimensions. These judgments tend to be particularly unforgiving (and hard to change) when people look or act in ways that are unfamiliar or inconsistent with what we think is correct. They also are terribly bad at incorporating situational information (remember the fundamental attribution error from chapter 5?).

The good news is, what we do with those judgments is our decision. Will we respond in ways that tear others down, make them feel worse (and quite frankly make the entire situation worse), or will we heed Paul's advice to let no evil talk come out of our mouths? This may ring true as a lesson from childhood, "If you don't have anything nice to say, don't say it at all." Yet, Paul is reminding us that we are called to more than that. Our words should build others up. They should give grace to those who hear. Grace to the people (or groups of people) you do not like nor respect. Grace to the people that grate on your nerves day in and day out. Grace to the person making mistakes over and over again.

Extrapolating beyond what is said out loud into the world of nonverbals, how might the standard of giving grace and building others up shape the way we think about our tone, our body language, our unwillingness to get close, and our eye rolls, mocking facial expressions, and crude jokes. These behaviors clearly are not building anyone up, so how do we tone them down?

Regardless of how people look, how they are acting, or the situation they are in, Paul writes that we shouldn't judge or despise others. Not only does Paul tell people to not look down on others, but also to not make people's lives harder than they already are. He says we should not be a "stumbling block"! Regardless of the way the other person is acting, regardless of our opinion about their life, we are called not to pass judgment, but to leave that to God. Our call is to "be kind to one another, tenderhearted, forgiving one another" (Eph. 4:32).

This might mean biting your tongue when you want to reply, "Well, what did you think was going to happen?" after someone in your family does something you think is stupid. Or perhaps when seeing the sink full of dirty dishes that are not yours, you could simply walk past them, or even just wash them—which increases love and patience in your home rather than bitterness and contempt. Little jerk comments and eye rolls are rife with contempt. Letting go of those "stumbling block" responses and replacing them with compassion, patience, and grace is what we are instead called to.

There is nothing biblical about looking down on people when they struggle, or fail, or suffer—even if they act like jerks. Instead, we are to love them and maybe even consider where we could learn from them. Martha had a great deal to learn from Mary after all, even though Martha felt like she was the one doing all the truly important work (Luke 10:38–42). Jesus models this for us as someone who humbles himself while exalting others (Phil. 2:1–11). Jesus is our model for the direction of our gaze. Rather than looking down on anyone with contempt or disgust, we should look up to them, admire them, see the good in them, and recognize the unique value they offer to the world.

LIVING FAITHFULLY

Psychology and theology both offer several valuable steps to help mitigate contempt that you can readily practice. We recently heard a story of someone who converted to Roman Catholicism. He said that one of the new practices he appreciates most is confession. At his first confession, he told the priest how much he hated a particular person. The priest's response was to tell him to pray for that person every day for a week. Who is your person? The neighbor who weekly blocks your car with their trash bins, the neighborhood drug dealer who strolls down the street one block from the local middle school, the obnoxious classmate who loves hearing themself talk, or the person at work who throws backstabbing insults like a major-league baseball pitcher?

Pray

Praying for someone we despise or hate can feel fake. It's likely that your prayer may begin, "God, I hate this person, and I feel justified in my hatred of them because they did the following. . . ." If that is the way you want to begin your prayer, go for it. If it's honest, it's the right prayer. The prayers of lament in the Bible are full of detailed descriptions of the wrongs people have experienced. But don't end your prayer there. Then pray for that person: pray that God would fill them with love and heal their (and your!) brokenness. Pray that God would help you see how the situation they are in might not bring out the best in them. Pray that God will give you opportunities to build that person up and to show them grace. If you don't know what to pray, you might pray, "God, I don't know how to pray, but I want to pray for this person. Send your Spirit to guide me."

Pay Attention

Another thing you might do is to take a week when you are intentional about monitoring your own contemptuous behaviors. Notice the sarcasm, the eye rolls, and the thoughts that pop into your head that demean another person or elevate your own value relative to theirs. Pay close attention to words or phrases like "disgust," "pathetic," "childish," "zero respect for," and "incompetent" that run through your head (or out your mouth). These terms are also associated with contempt and are a clear indicator that other nonverbal signs are present or not too far behind.

As a quick side note, now is not the time to start keeping a running track record of how someone treats you with contempt. This might get tricky. Once you've learned about contempt and its consequences, you will likely be highly aware when it is being directed at you. You are also more likely to see it when it is being directed at you than when it is acted out by you. This is not a fun experience. As you know, being on the receiving end of contempt is genuinely painful, and we hope that this knowledge can help you take steps toward changing unhealthy relationship patterns. One of the best ways to change how someone treats us is to change how we treat them, because your behavior serves as a model. Let us break negative cycles by taking the first step.

Gratitude and Appreciation

As Gottman suggests, one of the primary antidotes to contempt is gratitude. You could maybe start by writing a letter to someone you live with whom you know you treat with contempt often. You might tell them, "This is one thing I really admire about you." Name it, but also give examples of times when they were doing this; describe it in detail. The details are key. Don't approach this like you would signing a yearbook, "You are the best! Never change!"

You should aim for something like, "One thing I appreciate about you is your warmth toward our kids. I noticed you holding hands with our son, talking to him about his worries about the last day of school. You also went out of your way to listen to our neighbor who was just laid off. I am so grateful to be married to someone with such a caring heart." Then give them the letter. Simply naming the things we admire about someone can disrupt our patterns toward them, moving us toward the relationship we want to have. It also moves us toward the five-to-one ratio of positive-to-negative interactions that Gottman says we should aim for.

If you are feeling ready to take on even more, consider a gratitude journal where you try to list at least five things each week that you appreciate about a person you interact with regularly whom you struggle to "build up" and treat with grace. Whenever you are ready, share what you have written. As these thoughts become more habitual, it will likely change the way you feel about that person and make it easier for you to treat them in more loving ways.

Do Some Digging

Another practical step away from contempt is to consider a group of people that you tend to look down upon and spend some time researching what factors beyond their control affect their current life situation. Notice how this new information changes the way you think about them the next time you encounter them.

eight

LETTING GO OF A SCARCITY MINDSET

The plenty will no longer be known in the land because of the famine that will follow, for it will be very grievous.

—Genesis 41:31

Moreover, he said to me, "Son of man, behold, I will break the supply of bread in Jerusalem. They shall eat bread by weight and with anxiety, and they shall drink water by measure and in dismay. I will do this that they may lack bread and water, and look at one another in dismay, and rot away because of their punishment."

—Ezekiel 4:16–17

LEARNING FROM PSYCHOLOGY

Historically, prejudice has increased during times of economic instability or a lack (real or imagined) of resources. One poignant example is the traceable fluctuations in the type of language used in the United States to describe Chinese immigrants.[1] When unemployment was low and there was great need for workers to help build our nation's railway system, Chinese people were commonly (though not exclusively) described as hardworking and helpful. The minute the California gold rush was on, however, a sense of competition and scarcity set in and with it a dramatic rise in hostile, aggressive, and harmful sentiments toward Chinese people.

This shift can be seen in propaganda disparaging Chinese people and the United States' first ever piece of legislation to significantly limit immigration according to race or nationality. The Chinese Exclusion Act of 1882 made it impossible for Chinese people to immigrate to or become citizens in the United States. It was not repealed until 1943, and only then largely in response to international pressures to improve morale and relations with China, who allied with the United States during World War II. A careful look at US relations with China (as just one example) exposes what Mark Charles and Soong-Chan Rah refer to as an "unsettling truth."[2] In the United States, people of color were befriended by White settlers as tools for gain when help was needed but rejected when resources seemed to be scarce.

If we look closely, with an open heart, we will see that the same self-interested rhythms still affect us today, both on societal and personal levels. A primary and persistent culprit is the perception (and sometimes reality) of scarcity. Current conversations around immigration, for example, often become particularly heated when discussing whether immigration harms access to jobs.[3] The question of scarcity is grounded in the fear that there will not be enough opportunities for everyone. In another recent example, we see that individuals of Asian descent, broadly speaking, experienced an uptick in verbal and physical attacks during the height of the COVID-19 pandemic. Researchers have documented that when health and safety felt scarce during the pandemic, aggression toward people who appeared Asian grew significantly above the pre-pandemic levels.

Prejudice and a dislike for out-group members thrive on perceptions that there is not enough to go around. As a quick reminder, the term *out-group* is used in psychology to describe a group with which you do not identify. Because we personally identify as Christians, Buddhists could be considered an out-group to us. At the same time, Christians would be considered an out-group to those who identify as Buddhist. Thus, the terms *in-group* and *out-group* are always relative to you and your identity. These group identities form naturally and are the strongest when they relate to deeply held personal identities (e.g., faith, political views, country of origin), though they can be more trivial (e.g., Pepsi vs. Coke lovers, early birds vs. night owls). When we believe a resource is limited, we strengthen our ties to our in-group and begin to view those with whom we do not identify as "competition" or obstacles standing in our way of the resource we need, rather than as neighbors to be loved.

The most famous social psychology experiment exploring how in-group identity and out-group animosity form is known as the Robbers Cave experiment. A Boy Scout camp in Oklahoma, entirely surrounded by Robbers Cave State Park, created the grounds necessary for researchers to both create group identities and sow the seeds for out-group animosity as well. Researchers selected twenty-two boys to take part in the experiment. All the participants had completed fifth grade but were strangers to one another. The participants were selected to be similar in many respects, to prevent groups from forming naturally based on surface-level or easily identifiable differences. All the boys were from Protestant families, of roughly the same socioeconomic status and academic standing.

The boys were divided into two groups, the Eagles and the Rattlers. A series of ten objective activities, including baseball games and tug of war, and five additional subjective activities, including cabin inspections and talent shows, created an ongoing competition between the participants. Whichever team had the most points at the end of the full series of events would win the highly coveted trophy. Giving each team a name and a need to depend upon their teammates to win was enough to create strong in-group ties, which also set the stage for out-group animosity. As the competitions unfolded, insults were thrown like, "You're not Eagles, you're pigeons." A real zinger!

The situation continued to escalate as the Eagles tried to justify, or make sense of, their recent win.

> As the Eagles walked down the road, they discussed the reasons for their victory. Mason attributed it to their prayers. Myers, agreeing heartily, said the Rattlers lost because they used cuss words all the time. Then he shouted, "Hey, you guys, let's not do any more cussing, and I'm serious, too." All the boys agreed on this line of reasoning. Mason concluded that since the Rattlers were such poor sports and such "bad cussers," the *Eagles should not even talk to them anymore.*[4]

The researchers highlighted this last piece to show the physical distancing that was ultimately sought by the Eagles: a complete isolation between groups. In just two days, arbitrary and randomly chosen groups had formed strong group-level identities through a series of relatively low-stakes competitions for a prize that only one team could win. This in-group/out-group competition had created animosity, aggression, and physical isolation between groups. The just-world phenomenon, which we learned about in chapter 5, was also in full effect as the Eagles tried to blame the misfortune of the Rattlers on a moral character failing: their foul language and a lack of favor from God.

Additional points of heightened contention between the two groups were evident during meal times when "getting to the food first" and leaving as little as possible for the other group became a goal. Not only did these mealtime shenanigans prioritize the group (in-group favoritism), but they also promoted harm or disadvantage to the out-group (out-group animosity).

It might be tempting to dismiss this study; they were just a group of eleven-year-old boys at a summer camp, after all. But an impressive body of psychological research suggests that as we get older and the stakes get higher, this tendency to develop out-group animosity is only strengthened.

In one recent demonstration of this, researchers randomly assigned adults to one of two groups: a scarcity group or a control group. In the control group, participants were simply given $10 and told that later on in the study they would be asked to allocate the $10 between themselves and another person.[5] In the scarcity group, participants initially saw a representation of $100 but watched it dwindle down to $10 (think about seeing the amount of money in a clear piggy bank rapidly diminish right before your eyes). Participants were then told they would need to allocate the remaining $10 between themselves and another person at a later point in the study.

Knowing they had $10 that they would eventually need to distribute, but before actually allocating the cash, all the participants (in both conditions) completed a questionnaire that, as far as they knew, was completely unrelated to the money game they were about to play. The questionnaire probed the percentage of Black and White Americans that could be described by a particular trait, from 0 percent to 100 percent. We can try this for ourselves.

Draw a line (or tap your finger) on the line below to indicate what percentage of people from different groups could be described by each trait. Start by going through each word while placing your finger on the scale for Black Americans, then go through each word again, but with White Americans in mind.

What percentage of Black [or White] people in America are

Poor	*Hostile*	*Thoughtful*
Curious	*Loud*	*Criminal*
Uneducated	*Rude*	*Adventurous*
Courageous	*Musical*	*Grumpy*
Content	*Athletic*	*Unassuming*
On welfare	*Ignorant*	*Rhythmic*
Lazy	*Conscientious*	*Aggressive*
Dangerous	*Unintelligent*	

0% ———————————————— 100%

You probably noticed that several of the words encapsulate negative stereotypes often associated with Black Americans. In particular, six capture stereotypes around socioeconomic status, and six capture stereotypes associated with being violent or dangerous. The point of including this measure in the study was not to show that these stereotypes persist—this is already well-established in numerous studies. Rather, the researchers wanted to know whether the strength of the stereotypes differed for those who were in the "control" as compared to the "scarcity" group (remember the dwindling piggy bank).

Consistent with the notion that scarcity can breed hostility, the researchers found that scarcity can also amplify negative stereotypes associated with out-group members. Participants in the scarcity condition estimated that 64 percent of Black Americans could be described by the low socioeconomic status traits and nearly 66 percent could be described by the violent and aggressive traits. These numbers were significantly lower (56 percent and 57 percent respectively) for participants who had been in the control rather than the scarcity condition. The control and scarcity conditions did not, however, make a difference for how participants rated the stereotypical traits of White people. In other words, traits of one's in-group (most of the participants in the study were White) did not change significantly in times of perceived scarcity.

Although the researchers did have people allocate the money, to maintain their cover story, they did not report the results of the allocation task. So, we cannot say that perceptions of scarcity change people's generosity in the game, though there is other evidence to suggest that would be true. However, what we can say is perhaps even more striking. Perceptions of people with whom we do not identify become more negative in times of perceived scarcity or deprivation, even if those people have absolutely nothing to do with why there is a scarcity of resources. In the simplest terms, fearing there is not enough can make us more prejudiced.

Even more concerning is that our enhanced prejudice is not grounded in any logical connections between a stereotyped group and the dwindling resource. Those in the scarcity condition had no idea why the money available went from $100 to $10; there was certainly no indication in the experiment that Black people (or a single Black person) had anything to do with it. Further, remember that the participants completed the stereotype questionnaire while ostensibly waiting to distribute their $10. They had no idea who the person was they would be asked to split the money with. They certainly did not know the racial identity of the individual they would be allocating money to. Simply feeling like they were getting a small piece of the pie was enough for them to start looking (nonconsciously) for someone, anyone, to vilify or blame. Activating a sense of scarcity set the stage for more negative thoughts about an out-group.[6]

Part of the brilliance of this experiment is that participants in both groups had $10 to allocate. So it was not about how much money people had, or whether they had "enough." Instead, it was their perception of how big their slice of the pie was ($10 out of a $100 pie or $10 out of a $10 pie) that made the difference. In essence, when researchers created the perception of scarcity ("There was $100 and now I only have $10?"), they were able to amplify the negative social stereotypes associated with an out-group.

Imagine how much truer this is likely to be in real-life scenarios when the amount of a resource is fixed, people are working hard for it, and there is access to information about who is receiving the resources. Whether it is gold to be mined, a salary to be earned, a promotion to be awarded, acceptance at a prestigious school, or even just a buffet full of delicious food, if we focus on how what we have is a "relatively small" or restricted amount of the larger whole or believe we are entitled to the resource, we are fueling a psychological environment where out-group animosity and negative stereotypes will flourish.

Simply knowing we are likely to judge others with whom we do not identify more harshly when we feel like there is not enough to go around can be an important step toward loving others better. When we are starting to feel anxious, nervous, or afraid, like we might not have enough or a resource (or opportunity) is dwindling, we are particularly vulnerable to stereotyping others in a way that is harmful. Left uninterrupted, these heightened stereotypical beliefs can perpetuate the just-world phenomenon that tricks us into believing other people actually deserve to be in a less fortunate position.

Psychologically, we are not aware of any quick and easy antidotes to this phenomenon. The fear of scarcity runs deep. It activates all our survival techniques. Unfortunately, these techniques are rarely compatible with the Christian life to which we have been called. It is our hope that being aware of this phenomenon helps us all slow down and scrutinize our thoughts about others, particularly in instances when we feel like resources are being threatened. If we can be honest with ourselves that scarcity is making us feel scared, we can also remind ourselves that God loves us all equally and wants to provide for every single one of his children.

If we had to take an educated guess at what other strategies might be helpful to ensure that we continue loving (and not stereotyping) our neighbors, even in times of scarcity, it is probably most important for us to focus on what we do have. Reorienting our attention to where our needs are met or where we have a surplus may help us counter the scarcity narrative.

A powerful sermon entitled "A Mindset of Abundance" from Dr. Brenda Salter McNeil championed the power of gratitude as it relates to our trust in the goodness of God. Dr. Brenda's message suggested that we can adopt a mindset of abundance (even in times of genuine scarcity) because we serve a gracious God who has given, and will continue to give, abundantly.[7] How can you tap into this mindset of abundance for yourself? Maybe it is considering all the ways God has already provided for you and giving thanks. Maybe it is reading the Word and fortifying your heart with the promises of God to care and provide for you, to never leave or forsake you. Maybe it is simply taking the leap and saying, God, I don't know how we are going to make ends meet, but I am going to lean into your call to love others well and to give generously. Maybe it is reminding yourself that we are all God's children, and he isn't playing favorites. Caring for one another and sharing the resources we do have is a way we are invited to participate in the incredible work of God.

It might also be helpful to remind ourselves that someone else having more of something does not always mean us having less. We have a tendency to believe that your gain is my loss (sometimes this is referred to as a *zero-sum game*), even when that is not true. Many of the resources we rely on are abundant enough for everyone to have what they need. Rights and opportunities for you does not mean fewer rights and opportunities for me, because when someone gets an opportunity, they often have the ability to create even more. And many resources are renewable: if we don't hoard them by taking more than what we need, then we can all have what we need.

Human fear (and sometimes plain greed) is often what actually creates scarcity. One way this is explained in psychology is the *tragedy of the commons*. Imagine a field of grass and cows. As long as people don't overfeed their cows or hoard grass for future days, the supply could be replenished and all the cows in the community well fed. It is only when people start to panic and hoard the resource that all the other cows (and their owners) suffer. The cow story makes the point well, but it also illustrates what many of us experienced during the pandemic. The tragedy of the commons was alive and well in 2020 when people rushed to the stores to stockpile toilet paper, Tylenol, and baby formula. It was not uncommon during the pandemic to see people stockpiling these necessities, leaving shelves empty and new moms (and toilet paper users everywhere) in a terrifying situation of scarcity.

Was genuine fear (and not selfish greed) driving the overpurchasing? Almost certainly. Was this fear also ultimately harming others? Without a doubt. As is often the case, it was in these moments of panic that we also saw some of the most incredible examples of human kindness. New mamas created groups on Facebook announcing their willingness to share supplies of pumped breast milk or extra formula with anyone who needed it. These generous offers snowballed, and many who had the ability to breastfeed (something that is not a guarantee) or had extra formula quickly followed suit. These moves of generosity were not always even utilized, but they helped alleviate the fear of scarcity. They created a sense of assurance through a social safety net that all babies would have what they need.

Generosity sparked more generosity, and very quickly it was clear that there was more than enough for everyone. Looking back, it was such a beautiful testament to how communities can care for, support, and provide for one another both physically and emotionally (by helping to reduce each other's fears) when we are willing to be vulnerable about what we need, share what we have been given, and trust that God will continue to provide for our needs each day, resisting the temptation to take more than we actually need.

Yes, sometimes it really is a zero-sum game and your gain will be at my expense, but even then we are still called to share, give more than is asked of us, and trust God. Much of the time, however, it is possible for us all to have what we need and, if we are honest, many of us probably have a whole lot more than that.

Psych Summary: When a resource is limited (or there is a belief that there is not enough for everyone), animosity toward out-group members increases. Recognizing our tendency to deepen ties to in-groups and cast out-groups in a negative light during these times can help us ensure our sense of fear does not drown out our ability to love others well. How we think about others and the stereotypes we associate with them should be unfazed by what is and what is not available to us. Psychological research warns us, however, that this is not the case. If we aren't careful, we can begin to villainize members of our out-groups. These negative thought patterns can eventually facilitate the just-world phenomenon, or the problematic mental justification that other people actually "deserve" to be less well off than we are or have fewer opportunities or rights than we do.

THINKING THEOLOGICALLY

> Then Joseph said to Pharaoh, "Pharaoh's dreams are one and the same; God has revealed to Pharaoh what he is about to do. The seven good cows are seven years, and the seven good ears are seven years; the dreams are one. The seven lean and ugly cows that came up after them are seven years, as are the seven empty ears blighted by the east wind. They are seven years of famine. It is as I told Pharaoh; God has shown to Pharaoh what he is about to do. There will come seven years of great plenty throughout all the land of Egypt. After them there will arise seven years of famine, and all the plenty will be forgotten in the land of Egypt; the famine will consume the land. The plenty will no longer be known in the land because of the famine that will follow, for it will be very grievous."
>
> —Genesis 41:25–31

When resources like money, food, time, or love are scarce, or even if they just seem scarce, it brings out the worst in us. Joseph and his brothers are a case study of how people might treat each other when resources are scarce. If you remember, Joseph is the youngest brother in a large sheepherding family. His older brothers are wildly jealous of him. He is given a fancy coat representing his father's love for him. When this gift is given, his brothers suddenly feel that their father's love is scarce. To them, this also felt like the family hierarchy, where the eldest is supposed to be the favored one, is out of whack—status suddenly feels scarce. To top it off, Joseph has dreams of his brothers bowing down to him! If Joseph's brothers already had issues with jealousy and feeling like he was bragging, this pushed them over the edge. Not only were they jealous, with mean thoughts about Joseph, they planned his fake death, reported it to their father, and then sold him into slavery.

In the story of Joseph and his brothers, scarcity and jealousy make the story (and Tim Rice made the musical). Without their fearful thoughts about scarcity like "Our father doesn't love us enough," and "Our position in our family is at risk," that motivated action, there would be no story to tell. Scarcity appears again in the story when a famine drives Joseph's brothers back to him to ask for food, after he becomes an economic adviser to Pharaoh. The deeper story, however, is that God is with Joseph, and even when there is real scarcity in the form of a national famine, God still provides.

The lesson has often been preached, alongside Matthew 6:26, to just trust God when things are scarce and God will provide. Okay, yes, this is often true; however, sometimes it is not true and the very thing we need is not provided. That is the danger in this Christian message. We can mistakenly think, "If we just trust God when things are scarce, we will still get what we want or need."

What we think the real lesson in this story is, is that we should not let scarcity bring out the worst in us, specifically, our tendency to dehumanize others. Unlike his brothers, when things were scarce, Joseph still treated his brothers with respect and dignity. Even when his brothers came asking for food and didn't recognize him, he was respectful toward them and gave them what they asked for. At this point, many of us would probably not be disappointed if Joseph used the opportunity to tell off his brothers, but instead he uses the opportunity to reconnect with them. And not only his brothers, but his father as well. He does this by kind of kidnapping his other brother, but we can probably overlook this minor detail because he had no reason to trust his brothers after the whole fake-death and selling-him-into-slavery debacle.

Joseph is a model for us. Despite his brothers being the poster children for the "Rattlers versus the Eagles," he did not compete with or demean his brothers. Instead, in his wisdom, when things were scarce, he planned ahead, and he used his position to make sure there was enough for everyone, even his brothers who betrayed him.

LIVING FAITHFULLY

Psychology teaches us that scarcity—the fear that something is being taken away or the belief that there isn't enough—tends to bring out the worst in us. This can be true of how we treat those who are close to us, absolutely, but it may be even more insidious as it pertains to how we treat those we do not identify with or we deem ourselves to be in competition with to obtain a particular resource. Scripture, however, reminds us that God does not call us to give only out of excess or abundance. This reminder is grounding. It can be so easy to get caught up debating the details: Is there really enough to go around or not? This is the wrong question. Christ reminds us that we are called to give and to love anyway.

Identify your scarcest resource—time, money, job security, friendship, or perhaps patience? How does this scarcity bring out the worst in you? In times of scarcity, how might you shift to be like Joseph, giving wise advice, planning for the future, and acting with love and care?

Now, think of someone who feels like your competitor—whether they are aware of it or not. Perhaps it was a friend from childhood or even a family member, maybe a current colleague, a classmate, or another parent at your kid's school. Find a way to engage this person in a collaborative task, invite them to work on a project with you, give you feedback, or maybe ask them to be on your team for an event or game night. How does working together toward a common goal reshape your relationship with them?

Another thing you might consider is getting some true perspective on how much you actually have. Do some research on how much of the world survives on less than $2.15 a day or does not have access to clean water, religious freedom, or education. Our perspective of what we have (or what we lack) often comes from what psychologists call *relative deprivation*. We tend to compare ourselves to people who have more than us rather than people who have less. This creates a subjective sense that we are deprived and makes it possible for people to believe they are entitled to more or that they are disadvantaged. Zooming out to notice how many have less than you may help you to recalibrate and squash false or exaggerated perceptions of scarcity.

Finally, consider negative stereotypes about different people groups with whom you do not identify. You do not have to agree with the stereotypes; just make note of common stereotypes and their associated people groups. Now, ask yourself honestly, do you believe people from any of these groups are taking resources away from you in some way? If so, how might those beliefs affect the way that you think about and love these neighbors? How might these beliefs get in the way of your generosity?

nine

BEING OPEN TO THINKING AGAIN

Do not be conformed to this world, but be transformed by the renewing of your minds, so that you may discern what is the will of God—what is good and acceptable and perfect.

—Romans 12:2

LEARNING FROM PSYCHOLOGY

What is something you believe to your core? Perhaps it is how the land next to your apartment building should be developed or who should win the Grammy for the best album this year. Maybe you are deeply convicted about the conflict between Palestinians and Israelis or a recent political election at the local or national level. You may have proclaimed your belief on social media, attended a protest or rally, or even dissolved a relationship over this belief. Your belief might be about some of the most polarizing topics in the United States, like climate change, vaccines, immigration, or gun safety policies. Or perhaps you have deeply held beliefs about smaller things like cracking your knuckles causing arthritis, goldfish having a three-second memory, or sugar making children hyper? You might even be like one lady in Seattle who felt so strongly about the '80s music playing at a local gym that she started a locker-room campaign (with a petition to sign) to have the music turned off entirely!

Beliefs like these, even if they are small, inform our choices. We all have beliefs that motivate us to act, ones that we spend a great deal of time thinking about, or ones that we simply cannot see as a belief at all, but rather a fact or expression of the truth. What is one of those beliefs for you?

Write your belief here:

Now, we want to ask you something. Are you open to the possibility that you might be wrong?

According to psychological science, chances are, you are not open to being wrong. Even though you might actually be wrong. We could not know the chances that you actually are wrong unless we knew your belief and fact-checked it. If you look up a few of the beliefs listed above, you will find that cracking your knuckles does not cause arthritis, goldfish do not have a three-second memory, and sugar does not make children hyper. Are you surprised? It's okay if you go ahead and fact-check us on this.

We share this to illustrate how incredibly rigid our beliefs can be. On matters both small and large, we genuinely have a hard time understanding how two people could be so deeply convinced that they are right while holding completely opposite beliefs. And if this is true with small things like knuckles, goldfish, and sugar, which are relatively inconsequential, think about how much more confusing (and infuriating) it is when the stakes are higher.

The rigidity of our beliefs can divide us from one another, but it is not entirely our fault. Our brains are tricky organs, and they work hard to develop beliefs quickly and hold on to them tightly. This is particularly true when our beliefs are tied to any sort of moral issue, as many of our most tightly held and highly debated ideas are. Whether we are talking about racism, environmentalism, or religious freedom, chances are there is a moral imperative or a moral evaluation (good vs. bad; right vs. wrong) at the root of your belief.

Now, we are not here to talk you out of that belief, whatever it is—that is likely a futile endeavor. We are here to provide some insight into how quickly these beliefs form, how hard they are to change (even if you wanted to), and how that might get in the way of loving others better.

Let's start at the beginning. How do these beliefs form? The terrifying truth is that our most tightly held beliefs form quickly. So quickly, you probably don't even remember making a decision to believe that thing in the first place. Rather, it is likely something you've "always believed" to be true, is an "obvious truth," or "just the way it is." Consider the belief you identified at the beginning. How old were you when you formed that belief or it became important to you? Is it a belief that was passed on to you from an adult when you were a kid? Did you adopt that belief in your teens or early twenties? What evidence was presented to you, or did you seek out, that helped you to form and ultimately adopt the belief as your own? What counterarguments were presented to you, or did you seek out, as this belief formed?

If you are anything like us, this last question might have given you pause. What do you mean, counterarguments? There were no counterarguments. Who is actively trying to prove themselves wrong while simultaneously forming the belief? It seems odd, seeking out evidence in an attempt to disprove a belief as it forms. But when you really think about it, it is possibly even more odd that the beliefs we stake our time, our emotions, our votes, and sometimes even our relationships on were formed in light of one-sided evidence. And chances are, this is true for most of your beliefs. Don't believe us? Try to write down five reasons against the belief you listed at the beginning. If you are like most people, you won't be able to come up with five legitimate counterpoints to your own belief.

Let's try a shared example. Take, for instance, a belief generally accepted, that many of us were taught at a very young age: it is wrong to lie. You were likely barraged with a litany of reasons why lying is wrong and not a single argument in defense of lying. The point is not that we should be telling children that it can be good to lie; the point is that when beliefs are formed, they tend to be formed with only one side of the story. If you grew up in a Christian household, chances are you were not presented with a well-balanced set of arguments both in favor of and against the Christian faith. This is not typically how we teach people to believe. And our brains are used to this. We get a few pieces of evidence for a belief, and we adopt it. This is arguably problematic in its own right, but it gets worse. Once a belief is established, we are highly motivated to maintain it. Our brains are now in the business of confirming and preserving the belief. Let's unpack these two additional brain quirks together.

The *confirmation bias* is a tendency we all have to seek out and give our attention to information that confirms what we already believe to be true. This can take many forms. On a conscious level, we may actively solicit belief-confirming information. If you have ever found yourself glued to a single news channel that is aligned with your political beliefs, or completed a Google search looking for evidence to help bolster an argument or belief you already have (e.g., "reasons why lying is bad," "reasons to vote for X candidate" from your political party of choice), then you have fallen prey to the confirmation bias. Don't feel bad—we all do it. The most important step is being aware that we do it and having a desire to fix it. Actively searching for information that confirms our beliefs is relatively easy to address because we have control over the information we purposely seek out.

One way to address the confirmation bias, then, is to increase the number and variability of the sources you rely on for information. You could shake it up and decide, "On Monday I'll watch Fox News, on Tuesday I'll watch CNN." Or you could reframe your Google search or your conversations in a way that leads with curiosity about the arguments to support a perspective you do not hold: "What are the most important reasons to vote for X candidate of the political party I am not affiliated with?" or "What is the benefit of cracking your knuckles?"

Much to our surprise, in a quick search when googling the benefits of knuckle cracking, we came across an article that said that gently cracking your knuckles can temporarily improve your range of motion. A few minutes later, we had a growing list of evidence, including academic publications from computer scientists who have analyzed music from several decades and identified a lack of stylistic diversity in '80s music. Who knew! Maybe the locker-room lady is a gifted musician whose ears are bored. Maybe she is highly sensitive to sounds and loud music is physically uncomfortable for her. Whatever it is, these Google searches take all of two minutes and help to create some level of understanding about perspectives other than our own.

Can you imagine what might happen if we all took even this small step with our most tightly held beliefs? It might not change your mind (you might be humming "I Love Rock 'n' Roll" in this very moment), but the more you can understand another person's perspective, the less annoyed you might feel that they are campaigning for something you don't agree with. Seeking understanding with humility is one tangible step we can take to equip ourselves to love others, especially those with whom we disagree, better.

What is more difficult to counter with the confirmation bias is the way that we unknowingly give our attention to information that bolsters our arguments. If you believe airplane travel is dangerous, every single story of airplane trouble is going to leap off the page to you, whether you were seeking it out or not. And yet, you'll conveniently overlook the days when there are no airplane accidents to report. This is why it is even more important to be cognizant of the information we are intentionally consuming, because even if we seek out a balanced argument, our assessment of the evidence will be more closely aligned with what we already believe. The best thing to do, then, would probably be to anticipate this bias and be the most intentional about reading and listening to publications that counter our beliefs rather than giving our attention to information that confirms them.

In his book *Mindwise*, Nicholas Epley explains two problems of perception. The first he describes as a neck problem, and the second is a lens problem.[1] The neck problems are easy to solve, because once we are aware of them, we can choose to turn our heads the other way. This is the equivalent of choosing to do the Google search that might give you evidence to the contrary of your beliefs. The lens problem, on the other hand, is tough, because we cannot take off the lens (the eyes) we see the world through. In essence, some things we have control over. Other things we don't. We have to do our best to correct where we can to help minimize the consequences of these brain quirks that serve to protect our egos rather than connect with and love those around us.

A final related brain quirk is *belief perseverance*, and this is the tendency for our beliefs to persevere even in the face of counter-evidence. So, best case scenario, you are actively combating the confirmation bias, you are soliciting information to disconfirm what you believe, and you are actively paying attention to that information and trying to be mindful that unintentionally your brain is grabbing onto information that confirms what you believe. Even still, your brain is unlikely to budge on your belief. We know what you're thinking, "That is fine by me; I do not want to change my belief." Okay, we hear you. We know you don't want to change your belief. We don't always want to change ours either. But it's still important to know that once we have formed a belief, we may encounter ten good reasons not to believe it and that will not be enough to undo the five good reasons we had to believe it in the first place. God is not threatened by factual information about the world, and we should not be either.

Remember how we started this chapter, are you open to the possibility that you could be wrong? Do you trust yourself enough that you *would* change your belief if evidence pointed you in that direction?

For many Christians, one stumbling block to changing their beliefs is that we are relatively certain that our beliefs are aligned with God's. And, of course, we want to emulate God in all that we think and do. We will casually gloss over the fact that there are deeply faithful Christians on all sides of literally every hotly debated issue. We cannot be on polar-opposite ends of the spectrum and all be in perfect alignment with God's beliefs. So . . . how do we know if we are the ones who are really aligned with God's will and values? The following section will do most of the heavy lifting on this deeply theological question; however, there is some psychological evidence to suggest that we need to be very wary of our ability to discern God's beliefs. As it turns out, there is research on this question. Research that happens to have been conducted by a professor whom Brittany had the opportunity to work with during her postdoctoral appointment at the University of Chicago Booth School of Business.

We will warn you. You are not going to like this study. How do we know? Because at first we did not like this study. As a Christian, it can feel threatening. Hopefully by now you are aware that feeling threatened does not bring out the best in us. It certainly does not help us to be open-minded or more attentive to the needs of others. But we would argue that it is even more threatening to our faith, and our ultimate call to love others the way that God loves us, if we refuse to grapple with challenging information about how our minds have the potential to create God in our own image, rather than the other way around. This is especially tenuous when it comes to trying to discern what God thinks about something. So, here it goes.

The setup of the study is relatively simple. People were asked to reflect on their own beliefs and God's beliefs on a number of different topics. What won't surprise you is that there was a strong relationship between the two. If we are trying to believe what God believes, it is expected that the two should look similar. What was tricky, and particularly insightful about the study, is that the researchers intentionally manipulated people's beliefs. They wondered, "If we can change your beliefs, do we also change your understanding of God's beliefs?"

Mind you, these were relatively benign beliefs rather than the ones integral to people's identities, so they were a bit easier to manipulate. What the researchers found is that when someone was in a situation that altered their beliefs, lo and behold, God's opinion on the matter changed too (according to the person in the study). For example, you may be asked to report your beliefs and God's beliefs about the importance of recycling. Then, you would be in a situation where you read an essay about the importance of recycling. After the essay, you would report your (and God's) beliefs again. Not only would your views shift more in the direction of seeing recycling as important, but you'd also report God's beliefs as more in the direction of seeing recycling as important. This happened regardless of which direction people's beliefs were being shifted.

What is the problem with this? Well, for one, most Christians believe that God is unchanging. God's views do not change as a function of the information we receive or what we believe. It is concerning if we conceptualize God in such a fickle way. We should be striving to align our will and thoughts with God's, shaping ourselves to be more like Christ. We should not be changing our minds about something and then saying, "God probably agrees with me." Now, of course, there are times when you are wrong about what you believe and changing your views would put you more in line with God's. However, there are also times when your views are wildly inconsistent with God's, but you have the illusion that "God is on your side" and believes what you do.

This study shook Brittany initially because it made her feel silly and maybe even a little scared. It felt like the results meant "Christians are making God up." Upon deeper, and less emotionally reactive, engagement, we do not believe this is what the study was intended to claim, nor actually claims. Instead, the study is pointing out one of the most complex tasks that humans are asked to navigate: knowing what is in the mind of another being. Whether that other being is your toddler, your partner, or God, it is impossible to truly know what is in someone else's mind. Psychologists call the awareness of other people's minds as distinct from their own minds the *theory of mind*. Even though we recognize other people's minds are different from our own, it doesn't stop us from making these errors about what is in the mind of another person.

So, what do we do to understand the mind of another? We take our best guess. Importantly, our guesses, really our entire imaginations, are limited by what we have in our own heads. And what is that? What we know. What we believe. And so, even though it is unintended, we cannot help but conceptualize a God who thinks like us. There are two terms psychologists use to help us describe this phenomenon, which again, does not only play out with God. The first is *egocentrism*. We do not mean this in the "character defect," self-absorbed way, but in the way that humans have the most access to their own minds, and they are grounded in their own experience. It takes energy and effort to break out of that to take the perspective of someone (or something) else. Even when we do, we typically use an anchor-and-adjust strategy. Essentially, we say, "Okay what do I believe about this? God must believe something even more righteous than I believe." Our own beliefs are the starting place, and then we adjust our guesses about God's beliefs from there. The problem with this strategy is that it is always tied to our own egocentric perspective. If you've ever found yourself exasperated at not understanding the choice of someone else, thinking, "I just cannot understand how they . . ." you know this feeling firsthand. It feels impossible to unknow, unfeel, unsee, or unbelieve what we experience so deeply.

The light in all this, and the reason we have been able to come to peace with this study from both Christian and scientific perspectives, is that it helps us remember that ultimately, we cannot know with 100 percent certainty what is in anyone's mind other than our own. And when we are left with uncertainty, we tend to (unknowingly) fill in the blanks with beliefs and thoughts that are eerily similar to our own. While the brain uses this mental shortcut to keep us from dwelling in the uncertainty, it is not super helpful if our goal is to truly know and love others better.

If this is true for other humans, then how much more cautious and humble should we be when trying to understand the God of the universe? This is not an argument against pursuing knowledge of God. To the contrary, we hope it is an insight that can help us to know and love God better by recognizing that we can accidentally assume God's beliefs are the same as our own. Once we are aware of this tendency, we can put in place other means of knowing God that can help to protect us from artificially placing what we believe on God, and instead be more open to knowing God for who God truly is and being changed, rather than being the ones doing the changing.

Psych Summary: Whew! This section was a lot! Here is a quick recap. Humans' beliefs about the world form quickly with relatively little evidence. After a belief is formed, it tends to persist over time, even in the face of an abundance of counterevidence. For Christians, an added layer of belief perseverance might be that we all tend to report that God believes what we believe (even though we often believe different things). Why do we all think God is on our side? In part because when there is uncertainty, our brain fills in the gaps with what it knows about ourselves. When our beliefs are surreptitiously changed, we report God's beliefs as being different too. This doesn't mean we've made God up. It just means we have to do our best to learn who God is, separate from who we are or how it is useful and comfortable for us to view God.

While many psychological concepts are at play, the antidote to all of this is humility and curiosity. Without these things, we will likely find it impossible to love those who do not believe what we believe, especially in our current political climate. Simple strategies that help include reminding yourself, "I cannot be 100 percent sure what God believes." And asking yourself honest questions like, "When was the last time I looked up information to counter my own beliefs? Am I open to the possibility that I might be wrong?" When the honest answer to that question is yes, you are likely to listen more deeply and act with less judgment. And as it has been said, "Listening is so close to loving that most people don't know the difference."[2]

THINKING THEOLOGICALLY

> I appeal to you therefore, brothers and sisters, by the mercies of God, to present your bodies as a living sacrifice, holy and acceptable to God, which is your spiritual worship. Do not be conformed to this world, but be transformed by the renewing of your minds, so that you may discern what is the will of God—what is good and acceptable and perfect.
>
> For by the grace given to me I say to everyone among you not to think of yourself more highly than you ought to think, but to think with sober judgment, each according to the measure of faith that God has assigned.
>
> —Romans 12:1–3

John Calvin famously wrote that the human heart is an idol factory.[3] A famous atheist, Ludwig Feuerbach, critiqued Christians for imagining the perfect human family and then projecting that image onto God.[4] Perhaps we should not be surprised that the first two commandments are to not have other gods and to not make idols. Or, as Anne Lamott put it, "You can safely assume you have made God in your image when it turns out that God hates all the same people you do."[5]

As Christians we are stuck in a paradox. On the one hand, we seek out truth by reading Scripture, praying that the Holy Spirit will teach us. At the same time, we are imperfect (*fallen*, *imperfect*, *depraved*—pick your favorite word for human sinfulness) and are prone to make idols. When we read Scripture, we start with our own interpretation of what we read (which might be wrong, but it also might be right). One way we can make idols is that we assume that our interpretation is always correct. Another way we make idols involves the moment we think our interpretations are God's plan for how other people are to live.

So, how then do we read the Bible with humility? Are there ways to read Scripture, worship, and pray so that we can more closely align our will with God's will and "be transformed by the renewing of our minds"? How are we supposed to be faithful friends, parents, and employees who "speak the truth in love" while not judging others? Thankfully, the Bible gives numerous examples of things that needed to be reconsidered. In Acts 10, Peter has a vision that not eating a kosher diet is now okay. While this leads to a community-wide discussion and debate, it ultimately ends with a new vision for what marks a life of following Jesus Christ. One of the key pieces is that they spoke honestly with each other. There was uncomfortable disagreement, but they continued talking with each other and eventually came to accept that a nonkosher diet was okay—and if people wanted to keep eating kosher, that was okay too.

We have examples in Scripture of thinking again regarding concerns other than food. We also have examples of thinking again about interpretations of Scripture, and it is Jesus who is our example. If you read them separately, there are three different teachings in the Bible about divorce. These can be found in Deuteronomy 24:1, Mark 10:1–12, and 1 Corinthians 7. You are encouraged to read these for yourself, but here is a quick summary: Deuteronomy says, "Men can divorce their wives." In Mark, Jesus says, "Men, stop divorcing your wives." In 1 Corinthians, Paul writes, "If your spouse wants to divorce you, and you are a Christian and they are not, let them go."

These seem to be in tension with each other until we read a bit more into the context of each passage. The Old Testament teaching in Deuteronomy 24:1 allows men to divorce their wives if they do something "objectionable or indecent." According to this law, women cannot divorce their husbands, and the husbands get to decide what is objectionable or indecent. This law gave husbands a lot of power and women none. In the Gospel of Mark, Jesus is asked by the Pharisees to interpret the Deuteronomy 24 law on divorce. Jesus gives them an updated interpretation of this law and tells them that marriage covenants are binding and they should not divorce their wives according to their whims. While this seems restrictive in the present day, it would have been experienced as protection for women at that time. And then a few decades later, in a letter to the Corinthians, Paul interprets this passage again in light of the fact that Jesus is not coming back as quickly as everyone originally anticipated. Their question was "Should people stay married to unbelieving partners or grant them the divorce they are asking for?" Paul says that for Christians, the call is to stay married, but if the partner who is not a Christian wants to divorce, let them go in peace.

We raise these examples not to debate divorce but rather to highlight the fact that Jesus shows us how to think again—and when he does, it is to protect women who are vulnerable and being hurt by the religious law of the time. And then, modeling the same rethinking as Jesus, Paul shows us how to think again about divorce when circumstances change.

One teaching says to stay together and work things out, while the other seems to allow for divorce under certain circumstances. In these passages, Jesus and Paul are taking contextual matters into account while interpreting the same Old Testament passage. Imagine being a vulnerable woman, fearing that her husband might divorce her, listening to Jesus confronting the Pharisees. To her, this new interpretation would feel like loving protection. Imagine being someone in Corinth genuinely anticipating Christ's return any day, whose spouse feels trapped by your Christian faith. Would it not feel loving to receive the message from Paul that you can let these people go free and in peace if they do not want to stay married? Being open to new ways of thinking in these instances meant thinking through the big picture or the whole story in a particular context.

In another letter, Paul writes, "Do not be conformed to this world, but be transformed by the renewing of your minds, so that you may discern what is the will of God—what is good and acceptable and perfect" (Rom. 12:2). This passage tells us that the world would tell us that changing your mind is a sign of weakness. Instead, Paul says that thinking again, or being "transformed by the renewing of your mind," opens us up to discern God's will, the marks of which seem to be (according to the divorce example) peace and love. Openness to the possibility that we might need to think again requires humility that is only possible through the presence of the Holy Spirit. When we think again, we might just be able to love our neighbors better.

LIVING FAITHFULLY

For Christians, our beliefs are held deeply, so deeply that we sometimes prioritize them over the command to love. Our conviction and zeal can be so firm that it creates a barrier to loving our neighbor. The "cone of certainty" is a helpful tool to imagine what is most important to you and not open to rethinking, and what things are open for you to think again. The cone is narrow at the top, so there is space for just a few things; the bottom is wider, where you can list things you care about, but there is less at stake or maybe you could be convinced to change your mind on these things.

For Katie, the immovable truths at the top are the Triune God, the incarnation, and the resurrection; lower in the cone are things like divorce, women in leadership (even though I believe in it), theories of the atonement (there are at least four metaphors in the New Testament), and what happens during communion or the Lord's Supper. (Does the bread and wine change their substance into Jesus's body and blood? Honestly, we don't know. The Bible doesn't try to explain it, but denominations define their differences by their beliefs about it.)

Create your own cone. What few things are at the top, narrow and unshakable? What beliefs are lower down? If they are lower, who might you talk with who holds a different view that you might learn from? You might ask, What is at stake in this belief for you? Are there any people that are made more vulnerable or likely to be hurt by this belief? Does it affect how you live your day-in and day-out life, or just how you think other people should live theirs? What is the equivalent of "it's okay to eat nonkosher, but it is okay to keep eating kosher if you want to" for the belief you have in mind? What information would you need for you to change your mind on this?

Here is a drawing of Katie's cone of certainty. We encourage you to draw your own!

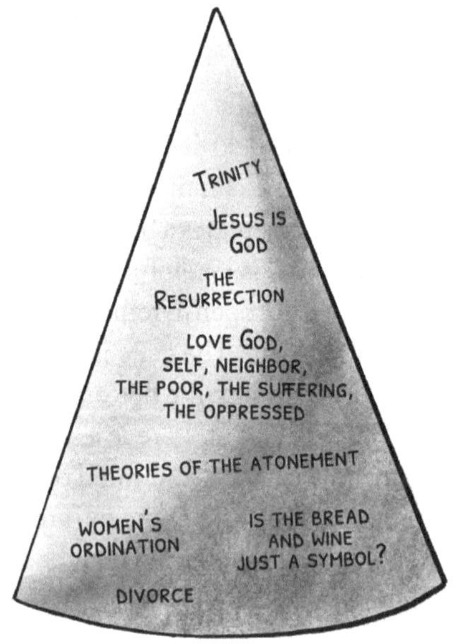

As another activity, you might find a friend and tell them the story of something you used to believe but now no longer believe. It might be something low stakes like a belief in unicorns or the tooth fairy, or perhaps something with higher stakes like your views about when life begins or whether or not the government should use the death penalty. As you tell your story, what was the catalyst that motivated you to change—was it meeting a person with different experiences, learning new information, or hearing a really good argument for the opposite position? After sharing this, you might ask them to share the same with you. What do your stories have in common and how do they differ?

If you are very brave and willing to be vulnerable, share about something you believe about God or the Bible that has changed. Again, what prompted the change, and what was at stake for you in your beliefs? Do you think your new belief moved you toward peace and love?

part three

CHOOSING TO LOVE BETTER

ten

TREATING EVERY PLACE LIKE HOME

"Reside in this land as an alien, and I will be with you, and will bless you."

—Genesis 26:3

LEARNING FROM PSYCHOLOGY

Where do you live? Would you consider this place home? Why or why not? We suspect that the amount of time you've lived somewhere and the number of pivotal life moments (e.g., graduating, landing a first job, getting married, having babies, adopting pets, buying or renting a first home) that have happened to you in a particular place contribute to what does and does not feel like home. One of the primary reasons time is so important is because it creates opportunities for familiarity. It takes time to develop encyclopedic knowledge of your local barista, find the best ice cream shop, and navigate a wonky gridless road system without a GPS. And if you're an introvert, developing that sense of home where you are known and know others can take extra time. Time in a single location, as it turns out, is indicative not only of how connected we feel to a place but also how likely we are to help the people around us (whether we know them or not).

When we think of being neighborly, we probably think about personality traits. We tend to think that someone who is neighborly is someone who is kind and helpful. And while we can't take personality out of the equation entirely, because internalized value systems do impact helping behavior, an analysis of sixty-five studies has demonstrated that situational factors are more important.[1] One of these factors is population density, or how many people live in a given amount of space. The more people per square mile, for example, the higher the population density. Another is *residential mobility*, how often people move from place to place.

Residential mobility is a question of how rooted people are in a particular location. High residential mobility is characterized by moving from place to place frequently. These transitions often happen independently, or with a small group of people, like your spouse or family, with considerably less attachment to extended families or broader community connections. Low residential mobility (sometimes called *residential stability*) is characterized by staying in the same place for a long time. This was illustrated beautifully in a TED Talk called, "The Profound Power of Gratitude and 'Living Eulogies,'" where Andrea Driessen speaks about her father who died in the same exact house in which he was born. This was striking, in part, because of the poetic beauty of coming and leaving this world exactly how and where you arrived, but also because it feels increasingly rare.

Much of the research on residential mobility is correlational, which is to say, it is limited in its ability to speak about "cause and effect," but it can expose patterns where things may influence each other. For example, we know that time spent in a location is correlated with a sense of connection to the place. Is the connection created by the length of time or is it because people already feel connected that they spend more time in a place? Perhaps it is something else entirely, like having substantial financial resources which make it possible to move frequently and also be less dependent upon, and thus less connected to, a particular place or group of people. Why is this important? Because if we want to understand how to love better, we need to know which comes first.

Correlational research shows that there is a relationship between helping behavior and the length of time spent in a location. Is it the case that more helpful people are also the same types of people that stay in the same place for a long time? Or might staying in a place for a long time actually make you more helpful?

While these possibilities are not mutually exclusive, psychologists can use experimental methods to test for causal connections. In one such study, researchers created micro-communities in a lab to see if the length of time spent in a particular location with a group of people affected their sense of connection to the others in their group, as well as their willingness to help one another. Researchers were particularly interested in two factors: (1) the length of time participants spent in a particular location, and (2) whether the person in need of help was likable or unlikable.

To explore these factors, participants were brought into a laboratory to complete a series of four tasks. The researchers cleverly manipulated the mobility of participants such that some completed all four tasks in the same room with the same group of people (residential stability) and others rotated rooms so that they were with different people in a different place for each of the four tasks (residential mobility).

The first three tasks were busy work the researchers did not care about to help make the experiment more believable. All three were independent tasks so regardless of the group (residential mobility or stability) that participants were in, they all completed the tasks silently and independently. On the fourth and final task, the only one the researchers actually cared about, participants played a trivia game and were informed that whoever had the most correct answers would win a $10 gift certificate to a store of their choice.

The researcher also announced that the group members could help each other if they wished, but reminded them that doing so would decrease their individual chances of winning the gift card. Those who had moved room to room (thus spending less time in the same place with the people they could help) were considerably less likely to offer their assistance relative to those who had been in the presence of the same people the entire duration of the experiment.

Adding a layer of complexity, one of the people in the room during the trivia game was actually a part of the research team masquerading as a participant. In the world of psychology, these people are called *confederates*, but we prefer to call them *fakes*. The fakes were trained to act in a particular way that made it obvious they were struggling to answer the trivia questions, but never explicitly asking for help. In half the situations this act was highly likable (think smiling and nodding), whereas the other times this act was considerably less likable (think sighing and eye-rolling). Surprisingly, the real participants were equally likely to help the fakes regardless of how likable or unlikable they acted, as long as they had completed all three tasks together.[2]

What this suggests is that when we are "stuck" with folks and feel connected to a shared place, we may be more likely to help them, even if they aren't particularly likable. Take a minute to let this sink in. Simply staying in the same place creates a situation where we are more likely to help everyone, not just the people we like. Consequently, a sense of rootedness and shared connection might help us to rise to the challenge of loving our enemies as much as our friends.

Another way of looking at this is that we are capable of helping people, even those we do not like, when we are "stuck" with them or we know we are going to be around them for an extended period of time. We don't know about you, but family readily pops into our minds here. We all have those people in our families we probably would not choose to be friends with or that we don't click with particularly well. And yet, we are more inclined to help them (than a random stranger) because we often can't avoid them as easily as we might like.

There are at least two ways to use this information in everyday life. The first takes into consideration our highly global and mobile reality. Travel is more accessible and easier now than it has been at any other point in history. It is not uncommon for people to move from place to place, city to city, or even country to country. Experiences that expose you to new places and cultures can broaden your worldview in many ways. At the same time, transience will likely affect how invested you are in any one place and how likely you are to help the people around you. Think about how likely you'd be to clean up a broken bottle in a park in your neighborhood versus a park you were visiting in a different city or neighborhood. If the latter seems less likely to you because it's not "your" park, it shows how a personal investment can change your willingness to act in ways that serve others.

When you're new to a place, you're more likely to be the one in need of help—relying on the kindness of others to help point you in the right direction, learn an unfamiliar custom, or communicate more efficiently. With this in mind, we might use these psychology studies on residential mobility to help us be a better neighbor when we are in new places, whether traveling through for an hour or settling in for a few years. We can do this by being more intentional about helping in the ways that we can (e.g., picking up trash or broken glass). Of course, as a stranger or someone unfamiliar with an area, we might not be able to help in all the same ways that a local would, but there are always ways for us to give or show our investment in people or places, to treat them with the same care and concern that we would in the places we spend most of our time. Even passing through, you still have a lot to give. Your kindness matters, and in situations where you may be less familiar with how to help, you may consider doubling down on the ways that you know you can.

The second potential application of this psychological research is perhaps a bit more challenging. It is an invitation to engage in some deep self-reflection when we feel the urge to move to a new place, whether a new church, a new company for work, a new school, or a new city. In some instances that may genuinely be the best (or only) option. In other instances, if we are honest with ourselves, we are running away from early signs of discomfort or disagreement. It is increasingly easy in such a technologically connected world to seek out and find like-minded individuals. While this may feel good (at least in the early stages, until differences inevitably emerge), it deprives us of the opportunity of loving those we are called to love. It also never gives us a chance to see what the psychological research suggests, that we are capable of caring for and helping those whom we do not like, as long as we maintain a shared location with them. What if being a loving neighbor is choosing to stay where there are other people you aren't particularly fond of, particularly because the act of staying is an act of loving that will help to maintain the elements of connection necessary for us to love others well. And after all, aren't those we do not like or are not loved by in return the very neighbors Jesus calls us to love?

Of course, not everyone moves around willingly. There are often circumstances in our lives that necessitate geographic and communal change. People who serve in the military, pursue education, travel for work, or are seeking safety, for example, may not have the luxury of pressing pause on their mobility. World Relief Western Washington is a Christian, nonprofit organization that does incredible work to resettle refugees and immigrants. Refugees flee extreme violence and oppression, and they depend upon the hospitality of other countries. Immigrants, like the ancestors of many present-day Americans, may be dissatisfied with religious oppression, political representation, job opportunities, or governmental policies in their home country and move to get a fresh start, greater opportunities, or a safer place to live where they can openly live out their faith. While your current (or next) location may not be your choosing, psychological research reminds us that your mindset and willingness to invest wherever you find yourself are within your control. That means that you can choose to be intentional about treating every place like home and challenging yourself to invest wherever you are as if you have always been there, or always will be.

Psych Summary: Staying rooted in the same place for an extended period of time can help you to feel more connected to other people who are also in that same location (even if you don't know or like them). This sense of connection can make you more inclined to help others. Two tangible steps you can take to love others better are (1) to stay, even when you want to leave, and (2) to treat every place (even those you are just passing through) like home.

THINKING THEOLOGICALLY

> Now there was a famine in the land, besides the former famine that had occurred in the days of Abraham. And Isaac went to Gerar, to King Abimelech of the Philistines. The Lord appeared to Isaac and said, "Do not go down to Egypt; settle in the land that I shall show you. Reside in this land as an alien, and I will be with you, and will bless you; for to you and to your descendants I will give all these lands, and I will fulfill the oath that I swore to your father Abraham. I will make your offspring as numerous as the stars of heaven, and will give to your offspring all these lands; and all the nations of the earth shall gain blessing for themselves through your offspring, because Abraham obeyed my voice and kept my charge, my commandments, my statutes, and my laws."
>
> So Isaac settled in Gerar.
>
> —Genesis 26:1–6

This is a traveling story about Isaac, and he is the picture of residential mobility. Unlike those in our contemporary world who move frequently for school or a new job, it was rare for groups to move unless they were forced to migrate due to war or famine. Isaac, however, was moving with his entire household of children, grandchildren, herds, and workers.

You probably remember that Isaac is the son of Abraham and Sarah, and the younger brother of Ishmael. Isaac is the one whom

Abraham was told to sacrifice on the mountain, but an angel intervened, stopping Abraham's hand. Isaac is the father of Jacob and Esau, twin brothers whose fights begin in their mother's womb. It is Isaac who, later in Genesis, will be nearly blind and near death, who will be tricked into giving the family inheritance to the second born, not the first, when he is fooled by Jacob in a disguise made to look like Esau. Isaac is a complicated figure.

There is a famine where Isaac and his family live, the second in their memory. God tells Isaac to go where he leads, not into Egypt but to Gerar, the land of King Abimelech and the Philistines.

The Philistines are notorious in biblical history, and this story in Genesis 26 is one of the earliest encounters between the Philistines and the Hebrew people. In this story, it is Isaac, the one in Abraham's lineage, who is interacting with them as he moves his family. The most famous Philistine is Goliath, of David and Goliath. Later on in the book of Judges, Shamgar kills six hundred Philistines with an oxgoad (a cattle prod) (Judg. 3:31). Then later, God gives the Hebrew people into the hands of the Philistines, to punish them (Judg. 10:6–7). It's safe to say that the Hebrew people will have a long and violent history with the Philistines. These are not the stories you would use as good examples in a book about loving your neighbor. The Hebrew people are the people with whom God has a covenant and as it turns out, their relationship with the Philistines can teach us a lot about residential mobility and loving your neighbor.

So Isaac settles in Gerar, among the Philistines. He farms, and his yield is one hundredfold, a very successful harvest. His success compounds, and he becomes very wealthy. Not only does he succeed in farming, but also in breeding animals. He has flocks of sheep, herds of cattle, and a large household of people. By all measures, he was very successful. And like many in his position, he became the object of his neighbors' envy.

This land that he moved to, Gerar, was formerly land belonging to his father, Abraham. Scripture tells us that as the envy of

Isaac's Philistine neighbors grew, they filled up the wells they were using for water, the wells that had originally been dug by Isaac's father, Abraham.

King Abimelech follows this symbolic action from the people with words, to let Isaac know that he, along with all his success, is not wanted in Gerar. He said, "Go away from us; you have become too powerful for us" (Gen. 26:16).

Surprisingly, Isaac respects King Abimelech's wishes and moves, but not too far. He moves to the valley of Gerar, still in the region, but on the outskirts of town. He found more wells from his father, Abraham, and re-dug them for use again. Amazingly, they found springs of water, despite the fact that these too had been buried by the Philistines during the time of his father, Abraham. The local sheepherders discover that the well is working again and tell Isaac, "We don't want you here either. This well is actually ours."

So Isaac digs a new well in the area and the same thing happens again.

So Isaac moves his people and his animals and digs yet another well, still in the area, but away from the initial two wells. At this third well, Isaac meets no opposition and says, "Now the Lord has made room for us, and we shall be fruitful in the land" (Gen. 26:22).

It is so interesting that Isaac was told by God to come to this land and yet, when he gets there, Isaac is guided by the requests and actions of the Philistines. Isaac listens to the voice of King Abimelech and the complaints of the sheepherders to help him find the place that God has prepared for him.

It is not until that evening when Isaac visits Beer-sheba that the Lord appears to him and says, "I am the God of your father Abraham; do not be afraid, for I am with you and will bless you and make your offspring numerous for my servant Abraham's sake" (Gen. 26:24). Then Isaac builds an altar and worships God in that very spot. They dig a well there too—because digging wells is their thing.

If you continue reading Genesis 26, King Abimelech comes to visit Isaac, and if this were a movie, it would be the buildup to a big battle. Abimelech comes with his adviser Ahuzzath and Phicol, the commander of his army. Isaac meets them and boldly asks, "Why have you come to me, seeing that you hate me and have sent me away from you?" (Gen. 26:27).

They reply in a surprising way. Not with another request for Isaac to move, or to take the recently dug well. They have been watching Isaac, and in his actions they see a love for the local people. They see he has moved when asked to move, and he gave over the local wells when he was challenged.

He acknowledged the conflict that his presence created by the names he gave to the wells—"Esek" (contentious) and "Sitnah" (quarrel). He did not fight with them over the land even though he believed God had brought him to the land. If anything, it seems that he heard in the conflict with the people God's guidance away from those places, until he found a space where his presence did not create conflict. What is impressive is that he invested deeply in each place; he literally dug deep wells. The wells were good for everyone in the neighborhood regardless of how long he and his household stayed.

Perhaps Isaac's inner dialogue throughout this phase of life went something like this: "Thank you, God, for all the wealth and blessings that you have given me. I don't know why my presence has been met with conflict, but I will trust that even in these moments you are present, maybe even in the voices of those who oppose me. And I won't let their frustration with me hold me back from being a good neighbor."

Perhaps with each new well, he looked for signs of God's guidance. Perhaps with each round of conflict he sighed and said, "I thought this was the place, but I guess not." It is not God's voice, however, that tells him to move; it is the tension he finds among the people who already live there. Unlike most who are wealthy, he listens to these people. He lets this conflict and tension affect him to the point that he is willing to move. It's inconvenient, it's neighborly, and it's faithful. Isaac doesn't fight the local Philistines with words or actions—he doesn't fill in the well with dirt, a kind of "Take that!" on his way out. He simply moves and digs a new well.

When his final well is dug and met with peace, peace with the local people, he declares that this is the land God has prepared for him.

Here is how this story ends in Genesis 26:28–33:

> They [Abimelech, his adviser Ahuzzath, and Phicol, his commander] said [to Isaac], "We see plainly that the Lord has been with you; so we say, let there be an oath between you and us, and let us make a covenant with you so that you will do us no harm, just as we have not touched you and have done to you nothing but good and have sent you away in peace. You are now the blessed of the Lord." So he [Isaac] made them a feast [a formal way to seal a covenant], and they ate and drank. In the morning they rose early and exchanged oaths; and Isaac set them on their way, and they departed from him in peace.

Isaac's servants dig another well that day and they name the place "Shibah"—meaning "oath" or "seven," the number of fullness or completion.

This is a powerful story of patience, loving your neighbor, honoring the history of the land where you find yourself, and treating each place you live in like home.

In this story Isaac could have claimed, "My father dug these wells, and even though you live here now, I have a right to this land." But he never makes this claim. It is as if he simply nods in acknowledgment and honors the voice of the local people, moving, and then moving again.

What would it look like for us to live in this way? To love our neighbors in a way that we are open to hearing their concerns, their complaints, even their requests that make demands on us? We cannot tell you exactly what this looks like in your neighborhood, but we saw this happen in one of ours.

About a year after they had moved in, Katie's new neighbors got a puppy. The story played out something like this.

> On our property was an overgrown holly tree. It had spikey leaves and little red berries. My husband, John, and I did not particularly like the tree, but with a new baby and two little boys, we had not given it much attention. After the puppy arrived, our new neighbor asked if we could trim the tree so that the berries wouldn't fall in their yard. The berries were a tempting and unhealthy treat for their new puppy. Our new neighbor texted this request to me and I sent it along to John, honestly feeling a bit irritated. They had just moved in. They chose to get a puppy. How was I supposed to control where the berries of this super annoying overgrown holly tree fell?
>
> That night John and I talked about the tree. I think our conversation went something like, "I do kind of hate that tree. But don't you think it's kind of a brazen request?" And John replied with something like, "I don't think it's that crazy. I wouldn't want poison berries from someone else's tree in my yard."
>
> Well, the next day I came home from work, and John had cut down half of the tree. It was taller than our house. He had rigged up ropes and a rock-climbing harness, because he is a rock-climber, and he was swinging around with a chainsaw with a giggling baby watching him from a car seat in the grass. The next day the entire thing was down.
>
> You can imagine our neighbor's reply. She texted, "Oh my gosh, thank you! I didn't mean you needed to cut the whole tree down!" When we met her mom later, she introduced us as "the neighbors who cut down the tree for Louie."
>
> What impressed me most was that John was not defensive; unlike me, he didn't think that was a strange or brazen request. He

heard a legitimate complaint and he immediately did something to address it. We had only lived here two years at that point, but he wanted to be a good neighbor. He embraced the inconvenience, he was neighborly, he was faithful.

LIVING FAITHFULLY

According to an article published in the *Atlantic*, the average American moves approximately eleven times over the course of their life (compared to an estimate of about four for Europeans).[3] Data also suggests that about 25 percent of Americans have moved in the past five years. How do you measure up to these statistics? Answer the questions below. If you are reading this book with friends, take some time to see if, on average, your group fits with the trends on transience described above.

1. How many times have you moved throughout your life?
2. How long have you been in your current location?
3. Of the places you have lived (if more than one), where did you feel you contributed the most to others, like your neighbors or the community more broadly?
4. What factors do you think played a role in your contributions?

If you haven't physically moved much, you might consider these questions in light of moving jobs, churches, or some other regularly frequented community.

Now that we have some context, we are going to invite you to imagine that you will never move again. In other words, imagine that you know for certain that where you live right now is where you would live for the rest of your life. This includes knowledge that your current neighbors are the neighbors you would always have. How does this idea of permanence make you feel? What about your current behaviors or lifestyle would you change? What would you keep the same? Why?

Would you spend more time getting to know your neighbors? Would you be more intentional about creating playdates for your kids? Would you spend more money locally, hoping that your contribution would help keep the businesses in your neighborhood thriving? We suspect that your answer is largely dependent upon how long you've lived in your current location. If you've been there a long time, you might not imagine changing much about your current behavior. If you've been there a relatively short period of time, there might be more you would change about your current actions.

Why? Because we are slow to invest.

When you aren't sure if the people next door will be next door in six months, let alone six years, it can be difficult to muster the time and energy to invest in building a relationship. If you knew those people would always be around, it might help alleviate some of the fear that you'd be investing into a relationship that would not last.

The issue, of course, is that Jesus doesn't call us to be neighborly only to those we know we will be with for a long time. Just like the good Samaritan, we are called to be neighborly even to those we are just passing by, to the folks we come across on our travels, those whom we may never encounter again. The challenge to us, then, is to not hold back. To begin helping and investing in others right away, to help like you will live (or work or worship) there forever.

Interestingly, the lock-down and travel bans that occurred during the initial onset of the COVID pandemic gave us a rare glimpse into some extra permanence or incentive to invest in the people who lived right next door. While some folks fled the cities for wide open spaces, others began to develop an even deeper sense of community with those in their own neighborhoods. There are countless stories of people who began setting up lawn chairs outside on the street every night to have an opportunity to "commune" with others outside. It was a time of deep connection and reliance on immediate neighbors that forged a familial bond.

Nothing was ever stopping anyone from having this type of social connection before COVID, but something about the sense of "stuckness" motivated folks to invest in a different way.

We can learn from these experiences. Not only is it neighborly to invest wherever you are, but it is also life-giving. You may be in a particular location for a short time or a season—a college student in a dorm room or a traveling nurse. How can you reframe these relatively brief seasons of life so that you invest more fully wherever you are, for however long you are there? This may look like treating the barista at a coffee shop you stumbled upon with the same kindness and financial generosity that you would tip the barista at your local coffee shop. Or it might mean finding a way to get involved in a nonprofit organization in your area now, rather than waiting to see if plans change or a move is on the horizon.

The call to invest where we are is not only about investing directly into the lives of others, but also about how we care for or tend to the places that we live, which can both directly and indirectly affect others. If you ever find yourself in Pike's Place Market, look down at the sidewalk paying close attention to the cracks between the cement stones. Oftentimes you will notice that the cracks are lined with tiny flower petals. Not flowers that are triumphantly growing through the cracks, but hundreds of bright yellow or pink petals that have been carefully packed together in the cracks. It is both charming and thought provoking when you realize that the petals must have been placed there on purpose. Stories that cycle through Seattle news outlets have suggested that it is an elderly woman who works to decorate the sidewalks in this way. It is a sweet and whimsical reminder that there are always small things we can do to contribute to the beauty in the world, wherever we are. Consider how you are being called to invest wherever you are by getting to know the names of neighbors, spreading flower petals, or digging deep wells. Do not underestimate the effect of your actions to care for the environment, picking up trash on a public park or beach, donating (rather than selling) used items, or creating a neighborhood free library box, an incredibly charming tradition that can be found in many neighborhoods across the United States.

It has been said (but not verified) that in response to being asked what he would do if he knew the world would end tomorrow, the reformer Martin Luther replied, "I would plant an apple tree today." What is one "apple tree" of kindness you can plant today even if you'll never see the fruit of that action?

And if, or more likely when, you begin to think about moving on to the next place, you might even stop to ask yourself the questions, "What would it look like to stay?" and "What can I do to dig a deep well if I go?"

eleven

STRENGTHENING YOUR EMPATHY MUSCLES

Love does no wrong to a neighbor; therefore, love is the fulfilling of the law.

—Romans 13:10

LEARNING FROM PSYCHOLOGY

Take a moment to imagine you are in a hotel with no internet access. Just like the "old days," you are limited to the entertainment offerings that are currently playing on the television. You flip through channels and settle in to watch reruns of a beloved sitcom. As the sitcom ends, you see that the next show playing on your current channel is a documentary highlighting the stories of children battling cancer. Interwoven are ads for nonprofit organizations requesting donations to support those affected by childhood cancer.

You have a choice to make. Do you change the channel to watch something else, or do you stay on the current channel to learn more? Be honest, what are you most likely to do at that moment?

CIRCLE ONE:

I would change the channel.	I would not change the channel.

After deciding, reflect on the reason for your decision by answering the question below in as much (honest) detail as possible.

The reason for my decision is this:

If you happen to be a fan of Christian radio stations, you might find yourself in a similar dilemma somewhat regularly. K-LOVE, for example, is listener funded, and a few times a year they run fundraisers to keep the station running. Even if you are already a financial supporter, you may not be able to listen to the stories of hardship and transformation that they share during these fundraising weeks without an overwhelming desire to call in and pledge even more money. So, what do you do? If you're anything like us, you probably squirm a little and change the station.

We know, we know, it isn't a great look. But, before you write us off, consider your own response to the TV question above. We suspect that like us, and the majority of our students whom we present with this same exercise, you indicated a similar decision to avoid the documentary. Most say that they would change the channel, or even turn off the TV altogether. They cite avoiding unpleasant emotions (e.g., guilt, sadness) as their primary reason. Occasionally they also point to financial limitations, knowing they could not respond to the funding requests. How about you? If you said you'd turn off the TV, let us help you sidestep a shame spiral. You are not a bad person for this response. It simply emphasizes how difficult it is to choose to empathize, because if we are honest, it is often emotionally (and otherwise) costly to do so.

Before you go down another (dangerous) road thinking that because of your response you either *are* or *are not* an empathic person, we would like to introduce you to some research on empathy. Jamil Zaki, a professor at Stanford who runs the Social Neuroscience Laboratory, has written about empathy in a book entitled *The War for Kindness: Building Empathy in a Fractured World.*[1] In brief, what Zaki walks the readers through is a compelling body of research that demonstrates empathy is not a fixed trait, but rather, it is a skill that can be developed and strengthened over time.[2] The catch? You have to be willing to sit in the situations that require your empathy. Unfortunately, much of the time people avoid situations that require the effort to empathize and so instead of strengthening this skill, they stagnate.

If you are eager to strengthen your empathy muscles, we are here to help. No matter how empathic a person you are, there is always room for growth in this area and we all have blind spots we will need to overcome. Besides exposing yourself to empathy-inducing scenarios, empathy can be learned or trained in several ways. Active listening, using the "I heard you say" method, is one way to do this. The principles are relatively straightforward, although in practice it is far more complicated than it sounds.

To strengthen your empathy muscles, when someone is sharing with you, you can respond in one of these ways:

- Paraphrase in your own words what they said: "I heard you say . . ."
- Invite clarification: "Is that right?" "What am I missing?" "Help me understand more about . . ."
- Affirm feelings: "It must be really hard . . ." "It sounds really overwhelming . . ."

Notice what you don't do:

- Share your own experience or suggest you know how they feel. It is important to sit in their feelings, not redirect to your own.
- Share any advice, solutions, or suggestions.

This second point, about not giving advice, is where so many eager-to-be-counselors psychology students have their bubbles burst. Several of them think (as most people do) that if they are "good at giving advice," they will make good counselors. Counselors are often trained to not give advice at all (although there might be times when they vehemently protest your decision to get a dog when you are already struggling to manage your life, so we are told), but rather to help someone hear their own voice through the noise.

Good counselors are not good advice givers—they are good listeners. Even once you know these techniques well (honestly, even if you teach them), you may still be bewildered to find how incredibly difficult it is to practice this in your own, not always pretty, daily life. One surefire way to see this for yourself: attend couples or family therapy! In these sessions, you will likely be coached through listening well. The real test, however, comes when your counselor turns to you after the other person has been speaking, looks you directly in the eyes and inquires, "What did you just hear them say?" It is almost comical how bad people are at responding. Why? It isn't because they aren't listening or didn't hear the person. It is because they are often listening to respond rather than listening to understand. The good news? We don't have to respond with all that much. Our conversations will likely go a whole lot more smoothly, and our loved ones feel a whole lot more seen and supported, if we simply listen for what their words are telling us about what they value, need, or feel. If we can reflect those things back to them and request clarification, we don't have to have the perfect solution (or retort), and we will save a whole lot of energy arguing about something relatively surface level, rather than the core (values, needs, feelings) of the issue.

Beyond indicating that empathy can be developed with evidence-based techniques and a willingness to exercise your own empathy muscles, psychological research has also begun to pinpoint how motivation can impede or enhance our ability to empathize with others well. One of the most compelling ways this has been demonstrated is in a set of studies from researchers at the University of Oregon. The researchers challenged the common trope that men are less empathic than women by demonstrating that groups of women and men empathize with equivalent accuracy, but only when they are equally motivated to expend empathic effort.

In the studies, participants (students at the University of Oregon) were asked to watch a video of another student who was actively applying to graduate schools. The video showed the student describing a recent personal experience with which they were struggling. Specifically, the aspiring graduate explained they had recently taken an important standardized test necessary for them to get admitted into the graduate school of their choice. Unfortunately, they did not perform as well as they hoped, and their score on the math portion of the test was insufficient for admittance to their desired school.

The participants in the study had one job: watch the video and try to accurately guess the thoughts and feelings of the student in the video, to truly understand what they were feeling and experiencing in that moment of disappointment. In other words, they were asked to empathize with the student.

When initially recording the testimonials about the disappointing test scores, researchers had asked the aspiring graduate student to note the specific times in the video they had the clearest thoughts and strongest emotions when telling their stories. Researchers then deliberately stopped the video at these key moments and asked the participants who were watching to write down what they believed the student in the video was thinking or feeling. Comparing what the participants wrote with what the student in the video reported thinking or feeling at critical points throughout the video allowed researchers to determine accuracy. The more similar the responses, the more *empathic accuracy* a participant was said to have.

Now, here is where the motivation piece comes into play. In one condition, participants were offered money for correct responses. If they were spot-on with what the aspiring graduate student reported thinking or feeling, they were offered two dollars; if they were in the ballpark, they were offered one dollar. If they were way off base? No money at all. Participants in the money-motivation condition could earn up to $8 if they accurately guessed the thoughts or feelings of the person in the video each time the video was paused ($2 at each of the four pauses).

In another condition, participants were not offered any money, but they still had to guess what their fellow student was feeling at the same four key moments in the video. These participants did receive feedback from the researchers about their accuracy that corresponded to the monetary tiers (spot-on, ballpark, or way off base) to keep the two conditions as similar as possible.

In a final control condition, there was no feedback nor any monetary incentive, but participants still had to guess how the student was feeling at the four critical moments in the video. Imagine taking a test where you would never receive the correct answers or a score about how you performed. How motivated would you be to put a lot of effort into your answers? Similarly, there was very little (if any) motivation to perform well on the empathy task for participants in the "no money, no feedback" condition. Because there was zero incentive, the researchers hypothesized that this control condition would have the lowest level of empathic accuracy.

The results? In the control ("no money, no feedback") condition, women outperformed the men; the women were more accurate. In the feedback and money conditions, however, no gender differences emerged. In other words, men and women performed equally. Something interesting is happening here. Why are men worse at this task than women unless they are given money or feedback? What the researchers suggest is that men may be less likely to expend effort to empathize unless there is an incentive for them to do so. The incentive may be internal, such as priding oneself on doing well, or external, such as a monetary reward, but one thing is clear—men are no less capable of empathizing than women. They just appear to need a greater incentive to do so.

Although it is tempting to magnify the gendered aspects of this study, the most important message applies to us all equally. Empathy is a choice, and that choice often requires motivation. We all have moments when we fail to empathize, or to empathize accurately, simply because we do not have the energy or desire to expend the effort. Remember the documentary you did not want to watch?

What motivates each of us to empathize in any given moment may be influenced by societal expectations, like the stereotype that women are, and are thus expected to be, more empathic. Or our motivation might be individual. Perhaps we feel it is important to be seen as empathic. When we are alone (as in the hotel documentary scenario) we might need to generate our own motivation for engaging our empathy muscles. One idea is to reframe these small choices as an easy way to train your empathy muscles, to get stronger by practicing empathy. This might lead to a donation, or it might help you be more prepared and better able to empathize with someone else that God puts in your path in the future.

So, we have learned that we are all able to grow in empathy and that our accuracy can improve dramatically if we have the right motivation. But why does this matter? Empathy itself is not the end goal—it is a means to an end. Empathy compels us to act; it drives us to love better. Helping behavior, as we have discussed, is often grounded in some sort of cost-benefit analysis, asking ourselves, "What is in it for me?" According to the *empathy-altruism hypothesis*, the only times when we are able to truly put our own interests to the side is when we are overcome with the emotions associated with empathy. In these moments, people will likely help no matter the cost. Jesus's sacrifice is perhaps one of the most beautiful demonstrations of empathy in action. Culminating in what is sometimes referred to as "the passion," Jesus's empathy for humanity moved him to action, sacrificing himself to set us free. Strengthening your empathy muscles matters because it is what precipitates acts of love and compassion.

What can be tricky about the connection between empathy and action is that we can be unknowingly fickle about when and with whom we empathize. We tend to empathize more readily with folks who look like us. This means we are more likely to help people from our in-groups (those with whom we identify) no matter the cost. This helps to explain research that finds Christians tend to be more likely to help people of their same religion but are not more likely to help, in general, than any other group of people (religious or secular).[3]

When people believe different things than we do or look or seem different from us, the process of empathy does not happen as automatically and we are less likely to reach the empathic threshold necessary to generate action. In these instances, when empathy is low, a cost-benefit analysis described by *social exchange theory* comes into play to determine if prosocial (helping) behavior is likely to occur. In essence, social exchange theory suggests that people will help if there is something in it for them. But of course, we know that these are not the only scenarios in which God is calling us to love our neighbor.

It is also worth acknowledging that motives matter. The personal benefits that come from helping others may seem subtle. Social rewards (e.g., the approval that might come from being kind to a waiter in front of a love interest) or the potential to be helped in return are two common forms of self-motivated helping. While we don't want to suggest you stop helping others if you are doing so out of self-interest, we do hope to challenge you to consider whether or not a love for God and for all of God's creation is really what is inspiring you to act justly or to treat others with kindness. If it is not your primary motivator, how might you ask God for eyes to see and a heart to feel the needs of those around you more deeply, so that you are overwhelmed with empathy and compelled to love, even when it is costly or inconvenient?

Psych Summary: If we cannot empathize with other people, we are very unlikely to help them. This is particularly problematic because we naturally empathize with people who look like us more readily than people who do not look like us. Luckily, we can cultivate empathy. While there are many ways to strengthen your empathy muscles, two discussed here include finding your motivation for empathizing and choosing to stay in situations that require empathy to strengthen your empathy muscles.

THINKING THEOLOGICALLY

In letters that circulated after Jesus's death and resurrection, the Christian community was trying to figure out how to live together, in actual unity. They wanted to figure out how they were to live together, both those who had been following the Jewish lifestyle codes and the new converts who had never been Jewish. Questions included topics such as these: What should we eat? How should we live with each other? Which Jewish laws should we retain? How should those who are rich share their wealth with those who are poor? One theme resounded in all these letters regardless of the topic being discerned: love. And this love involved feeling empathy toward others as well as doing right by their neighbors by alleviating their suffering and working toward peaceful relationships. This is demonstrated in the following letters:

> Finally, all of you, have unity of spirit, sympathy, love for one another, a tender heart, and a humble mind.
>
> —1 Peter 3:8

> Bear one another's burdens, and in this way you will fulfill the law of Christ.
>
> —Galatians 6:2

> For he is our peace; in his flesh he has made both groups into one and has broken down the dividing wall, that is, the hostility between us.
>
> —Ephesians 2:14

> Love does no wrong to a neighbor; therefore, love is the fulfilling of the law.
>
> —Romans 13:10

A new interpretation of the law is simply to act with love. How will the new group following Jesus be known? In John 13:35, Jesus tells them, "By this, they will know that you are my disciples, that you love each other." One way to interpret these passages is that we should love and care for "our people" (i.e., our fellow Christians) as a witness to a different way to live. The focus of this kind of love is that it is contagious and others will want to convert to being a Christian to experience this type of loving community. With this way of thinking, the in-group remains the in-group and we fail to love the out-group unless they convert and join us. Based on what we learned above, this is having empathy for those who are like us.

While our love and care should be a witness, the goal is not to do this to make others jealous or want "in," but to try to have a different kind of love-marked relationship with each person who exists. When this is done mutually, when people who are not in the same social groups love and care for one another, a different kind of community is formed—and it stands out. This is the type of community Paul is encouraging people to have. He recognizes that until Jesus came along they belonged to different groups. But now, they all follow Jesus—it's the one thing they have in common. And how does Jesus tell them to set themselves apart? Not with T-shirts or their political affiliation or their position on a certain issue, but with love. Love should set them apart.

Then we have stories like the good Samaritan, where Christian love is not merely about loving other Christians, but to love those who are outsiders, especially those who are outsiders or possibly even our enemies. If you have read *Gilead* by Marilynne Robinson, this is how the main character loves his namesake neighbor, Jack. Jack is the type of kid who is called to the principal's office regularly, is known for making poor choices, is a bad influence on his peers, and is a generally unethical kid. The brilliance of Robinson's writing is how perfectly she captures the human struggle to love someone who is so frustrating. One lesson from psychology is that if our motivation to help others comes from what we get out of it, rather than how much empathy we have for them, we are less likely to help. But if we make a genuine effort to empathize with someone whom we find frustrating or who is different from us, we can empathize and actually begin to fulfill Jesus's call to his disciples to be a community marked by love.

Empathy is really all about love, letting our hearts hurt or break with the pain of others, not just our own pain. Paul puts it well in his letter to the Ephesians. He tells them that they want to divide themselves, or remain divided, but following Jesus means that we recognize that he has already brought down any dividing wall we have built.

> So then, remember that at one time you Gentiles by birth, called "the uncircumcision" by those who are called "the circumcision"—a physical circumcision made in the flesh by human hands—remember that you were at that time with-

> out Christ, being aliens from the commonwealth of Israel, and strangers to the covenants of promise, having no hope and without God in the world. But now in Christ Jesus you who once were far off have been brought near by the blood of Christ. For he is our peace; in his flesh he has made both groups into one and has broken down the dividing wall, that is, the hostility between us. He has abolished the law with its commandments and ordinances, so that he might create in himself one new humanity in place of the two, thus making peace, and might reconcile both groups to God in one body through the cross, thus putting to death that hostility through it. So he came and proclaimed peace to you who were far off and peace to those who were near; for through him both of us have access in one Spirit to the Father. So then you are no longer strangers and aliens, but you are citizens with the saints and also members of the household of God, built upon the foundation of the apostles and prophets, with Christ Jesus himself as the cornerstone. In him the whole structure is joined together and grows into a holy temple in the Lord; in whom you also are built together spiritually into a dwelling place for God.
>
> —Ephesians 2:11–22

It's easier and certainly more comfortable to turn away from the pain or frustration of other people, especially when they are different from us and even more so when we find them frustrating or annoying. As this passage notes, however, Christ has broken down the walls that we have built to divide ourselves. Jesus has reconciled us to one another and the way that we live into that truth is to love one another. As the research shows, we can choose to be more loving, more empathic. Our motivation can be Jesus's and Paul's teaching that this is the way we are supposed to live—and we can practice this alongside others, who are also seeking to be known as his disciples by their love. When we love one another, we are fulfilling the law (Rom. 13:10).

LIVING FAITHFULLY

Since we now know that you can make a choice to empathize just by putting in some time and effort, let's try it out. The typical reaction to encountering pain is to avoid it, whether it's our own pain or the pain of another. Insights from psychology and theology teach us that one way we can be a good neighbor is to move toward the pain of others. One way to do this is to begin to listen to stories of pain or suffering. Here are some ways you can move toward the pain of others and strengthen your empathy muscles by reading, listening, watching, and talking:

- Read something that makes you sad. Maybe it's a story about families affected by the latest shooting in America or the local news story about poverty in your neighborhood.
- Listen to someone in pain. The next time someone begins to tell you that they have had a rough week, ask them to join you for a cup of tea so you can listen to what made their week so hard.
- Learn about the lives of people who are in your out-group. This week you could watch a movie like *CODA*, which tells the story of the deaf community in a hearing world. Movies like this can help you understand their beautiful lives, as well as the challenges faced by deaf people in a hearing world.
- Go talk to someone you find annoying. Instead of running back inside after you take out your trash, engage them in a conversation, ask how their day was or what they think about the new bike lanes in your neighborhood. You might talk with the parent of the kid who is creating problems in your kid's class to find out more about their story. Take what you learn as an invitation to grow in knowledge and empathy. For example, if you learn that they are navigating neurodivergence, like an ADHD diagnosis, take some time to ask questions about what that is like or find a book to read that can help you to understand their experience more fully.

- Let empathy move you to action. When you begin to experience empathy, let it fuel you to loving actions. It might mean you consider the resources you do have to give to a worthy cause or to directly help someone God has placed in your path. This doesn't have to be money (though of course it could be); it could be your time, your talents and knowledge, or even your voice.

Be warned, once you start to do this, your heart will likely grow or be broken by the vulnerability and challenging realities your neighbors are facing. It can even start to get overwhelming because we have access to information about the amount of brokenness and pain on a global rather than simply a local scale. Give yourself permission to do one thing a day to intentionally build your empathy muscles. You may even decide to focus on one issue at a time. At the end of the day or week, ask yourself, What did I do to grow in empathy today? How did I let empathy move me to action this week? We don't have to do everything, and if we let ourselves get overwhelmed, it is likely that we will do nothing. You can focus on one thing at a time. Trust that God will use your yes to love others well.

twelve

TALKING LESS AND LISTENING MORE

Be quick to listen, slow to speak.

—James 1:19

LEARNING FROM PSYCHOLOGY

If you are reading this book, chances are you care a lot about other people and you want to find ways to love them better. No one picks up a book on neighbor love if they have zero intention of trying to grow in their love for others. And yet, it is not uncommon for us to choose our own comfort over an opportunity to love someone else.

Consider the last time you were in a public transit situation—riding a bus, train, plane, or perhaps even in the back of a taxicab or Lyft. Can you picture a single face of one of the people you were traveling with? Did you speak to any of them? What was the conversation like? Was it fun? Insightful?

Ben Rector and Alicia Keys have both produced powerful songs about these types of everyday public exchanges. Both "The Men That Drive Me Places" and "Underdog" pay tribute to the incredible people and stories you can come to know if you simply take the time to talk to the person sitting in the front seat of your taxi.

Keys's lyrics beautifully capture the power of these conversations to transform us if only we are willing to engage:

> One conversation, a single moment.
> The things that change us if we notice.
> When we look up sometimes.

But how many of us, if we are honest, take the time to hear the stories of the people we sit or stand across from? In fact, we were recently horrified to learn that there is a setting on Lyft and Uber applications that allows you to set "no conversation" preferences, informing the driver ahead of time that you do not want to chat. Even if you never utilize this feature, how often do you actually make small talk with a cab driver or someone standing next to you in the grocery line? For many of us, the numbers are probably quite dismal. And this is true even though we earnestly want to love all God's children. It is probably also true even though you have personally experienced the emotional benefits that come from even the smallest of exchanges with other people. If you've ever caught yourself smiling walking away from an unplanned conversation with a stranger, you know what we mean.

Juliana Schroeder and Nicholas Epley are the authors of an impressive set of studies that demonstrate the positive impact that talking to strangers (gasp) has on our happiness.[1] Recently, Schroeder gave a fabulous TED Talk summarizing this work and linking it to the epidemic of loneliness we are currently experiencing in the United States.[2] We encourage you to look it up to hear about these studies in her own words, but for now, we will give you a quick summary.

People in Chicagoland going about their daily commutes (in buses and trains) were approached and asked to take part in a study. Participants who agreed were given instructions for their public commute. Specifically, the instructions prompted them to do one of three things.

1. Please keep to yourself and enjoy your solitude on the train today. Take this time to sit alone with your thoughts. Your goal is to focus on yourself and the day ahead of you.
2. Please have a conversation with a new person on the train today. Try to make a connection. Find out something interesting about him or her and tell them something about you. The longer the conversation, the better. Your goal is to try to get to know your community neighbor this morning.
3. Please do not make any changes to your normal commute. Your goal is to do as you would normally do.

Participants were also given a stamped envelope with a survey and a $5 gift card. They were told to follow their instructions for their commute and at the end of their commute to complete the survey and mail it back to the researchers. The survey probed how happy participants felt after their commute and how productive their commute was relative to normal. Researchers found that participants who were instructed to talk to a stranger reported being happier but no less productive than those who were asked to sit in solitude.

If talking to strangers can make us happier, why don't we do it more often?

Luckily, Schroeder and Epley tackled this question as well. What they found was that a lack of spontaneous interactions with strangers on public transit likely stems from at least two things. First, people tend to mispredict the condition that will make them feel happier. When simply asked to guess which set of instructions would result in the more pleasant commute—solitude or a conversation with a stranger—the majority predicted the solitude condition to result in greater happiness. In other words, people predicted the opposite of what the researchers actually found.

Another interesting cognitive barrier that the researchers identified is that people often believe others do not want to talk with them. This is particularly true for people who are less inclined naturally to engage in spontaneous conversations with strangers.

Instead, it might be helpful to recognize that if social connection can make us happier, it will likely make someone else happier too. This is likely even more true if the conversation gives someone an opportunity to share details about themselves or their own life, an activity that neuroscientists Diana Tamir and Jason Mitchell have identified activates common reward networks in the brain.[3] Actually, Tamir's work goes one step further and shows that not only is talking about one's self rewarding, people are actually willing to lose money in an experiment to answer questions about themselves. If people will pay to talk about themselves in an experiment, it feels like a pretty safe bet that they would be delighted to have a stranger (like you!) take an interest in them and ask them questions. Who wouldn't want to feel visible (rather than invisible) and worthy of being known (rather than unworthy of any attention)?

Psych Summary: People predict that it would be more pleasant to sit in solitude for a commute than to try to strike up a conversation with a stranger. Research suggests they are wrong. Talking to strangers while commuting and taking the time to get to know them actually makes us feel happier and no less productive. Mispredictions about how happy we will feel after talking to a stranger is one barrier. Another is how quickly we capitulate to the social norms of silence we witness on buses and trains. We expect that other people do not want to talk to us, and so we rarely engage. What if, instead, we believed that we could make someone else's day happier by talking to them? How might that change the way we approach our daily commutes or the time we stand in line next to strangers? Remember, the people in our given environment at any given place and time, they are our neighbors.

THINKING THEOLOGICALLY

> If then there is any encouragement in Christ, any consolation from love, any sharing in the Spirit, any compassion

and sympathy, make my joy complete: be of the same mind, having the same love, being in full accord and of one mind. Do nothing from selfish ambition or conceit, but in humility regard others as better than yourselves. Let each of you look not to your own interests, but to the interests of others. Let the same mind be in you that was in Christ Jesus,

who, though he was in the form of God,
did not regard equality with God
as something to be exploited,
but emptied himself,
taking the form of a slave,
being born in human likeness.
And being found in human form,
he humbled himself
and became obedient to the point of death—
even death on a cross.

—Philippians 2:1–8

Writing to those living in Philippi, Paul says that those who share in the life of the Spirit, who are encouraged by Christ, should have unity in mind and love. This way of living is humble, and the path to unity is to look to the "interests of others." To be humble, to listen to others is to become like Christ. This passage encourages us to admire other people, even celebrate the ways they are better than us. While we may not always know how strangers are better than us, we can certainly be intentional about acknowledging the good in them we do see. If you see another mom doing a great job navigating her toddler's meltdown when they have to leave the park, or a classmate you don't know well who gives a great presentation, make it a point to share your admiration with them. These compliments cost you nothing, but they can make someone else feel seen and celebrated.

Philosopher and mystic Simone Weil, who became a famous theologian because of her simple yet profound reflections on faith, wrote, "Attention is the purest and rarest form of generosity." She also wrote, "Attention, taken to its highest degree, is the same thing as prayer. It presupposes faith and love. Absolutely unmixed attention is prayer."[4] To listen to others with unmixed attention is to pray for them, to love them. One particularly challenging part of this is "with unmixed attention." Even if your phone is put away, you may struggle to be in the moment instead of thinking about the next event you need to drive your kids to, whether or not you paid your most recent medical bill, or what is taking your crush so long to respond to your text.

Certain spaces can help us to create unmixed attention. Ever sat in an inflatable not-quite-big-enough-for-four hot tub or been without cell phone service on a long hike? These types of experiences are rare opportunities to be close to one another and just talk and listen. There is really nothing else to do in these moments except to give our unmixed attention to one another. When the people we are with are close friends or family, it is easy for us to see how precious this time can be. But what about if it was a stranger? Why not seize other moments of inescapable closeness (like the four-hour flight next to a complete stranger or the forty-minute wait at the DMV) and treat them as an opportunity to give someone your undivided attention rather than logging an extra few hours of screen time for the week?

The womanist theologian Delores Williams says that one of the ways our society harms Black women specifically, but people generally, is to make them invisible. She uses the word *invizibilize* for this phenomenon. This can happen through stereotypes on the societal level, but it can also happen in small ways when we ignore or fail to see one another. To oppose this force, she suggests affirming the *somebodiness* of each person.[5] Each person is unique, a somebody who has experiences, perspective, and wisdom that is all their own. To listen to another person with genuine curiosity and openness to what they might teach you is to disrupt *invizibilizing* patterns in our society. Seeing the unique, quirky, inspiring details of another person and hearing their life story, their perspective on things, their beliefs and opinions, are two of the ways to listen more and talk less in order to love better.

LIVING FAITHFULLY

Look up Ben Rector's song "The Men That Drive Me Places" or Alicia Keys's song "Underdog." Listen to one or both carefully, and answer the questions below:

---

1. What does the song bring up for you?

2. What do we learn about the taxicab drivers in the songs that helps you to humanize them or appreciate their "somebody-ness"?

3. In what ways might the act of talking to a stranger in a taxicab, a bus, or a line at Starbucks be an act of neighborly love?

4. In what ways might ignoring the person driving a taxicab be dehumanizing or invisibilizing?

5. Have you ever been transformed or positively affected by a conversation with a stranger?

6. If you are someone who doesn't talk to strangers often, which of the two explanations offered in the research experiment best describes your own resistance?

    a. I don't think I will enjoy the conversation.
    b. I don't think the other person wants to talk to me.

7. In what ways has this chapter challenged that belief for you?

Now that you've had a chance to reflect, it is time to take the plunge. As you go throughout your week, we encourage you to go out and talk to strangers. Better yet, go out and listen to them.

If you're an introvert and you are actively cringing just thinking about this challenge, then let us give you a tip. It can be really helpful to have a mental script that you can use as an on-ramp for social conversations. A good excuse to start a conversation goes a long way. Feel free to use this book as your excuse. It could be something as simple as, "I'm reading this book that assigns me different challenges. I'm wondering if you'd be willing to share a moment of joy that you experienced this week?"

The next time you are standing in a checkout line, riding a bus, or throwing a ball at the dog park, you could casually strike up a conversation with someone nearby. If you need additional prompts, you could start with these questions:

- What is your favorite thing to do in this area?
- Do you have a favorite restaurant in this neighborhood?
- What was your neighborhood like growing up?

- What is the best advice you've ever received?
- What accomplishment are you most proud of in your life so far?
- What is something that made you laugh this week?
- Are you reading any good books or watching any TV shows you are really enjoying? Tell me what you like about it.
- Would you be willing to share a time when someone surprised you in a way that made you feel extra loved or cared for?

Get creative with it and make the questions your own. This is not only a fun way to love others but, according to the research, it will also bring some joy into your own life.

thirteen

EMBRACING THE POWER OF YOUR PRESENCE

Praise be to the God and Father of our Lord Jesus Christ, the Father of compassion and the God of all comfort, who comforts us in all our troubles, so that we can comfort those in any trouble with the comfort we ourselves receive from God.

—2 Corinthians 1:3–4 NIV

LEARNING FROM PSYCHOLOGY

As we are learning, the desire to love others is only part of the battle. We regularly have to get out of our own way and out of our own comfort zones to do this well. Sometimes this means being willing to start a conversation. Other times this means being willing to sit silently with those who hurt.

Reflecting on the stages of helping from chapter 2, we zoomed in on the idea that oftentimes people fail to help because they do not know what to do, or they are unsure what would be helpful. This is a very real fear. Life is complex, and we do not have all (if any) of the solutions, especially not for someone else. In this chapter, we want to suggest to you that loving your neighbor can be simple, even though it might not be easy. Specifically, we want to help you focus on the power of your presence, what it looks like to show up and just be with other people. Doing so can reduce the pain they experience, even when we can't solve or entirely remove their pain.

To make such a strong claim about being able to reduce others' pain with our presence, psychologists have to do something a bit unorthodox: They have to intentionally put people in pain under different social conditions. Don't worry, the studies we will discuss have been approved by an ethics committee. Everyone willingly agreed to participate, and all had the right to withdraw at any point in time.

While psychologists have several tools up their sleeves to induce pain (e.g., hot sauce taste tests, air horns, ice baths for your hands), one recent social neuroscience study relied on a thermal pain-inducing procedure.[1] Researchers applied heat to participants' left forearms for seven seconds at a time. The study began with a pain calibration trial exposing participants to heat ranging from 109.4 to 116.6 degrees Fahrenheit and asking participants to rate the pain. These initial trials allowed the researchers to determine an individual participant's sixty out of one hundred on a pain scale. The temperature corresponding to each person's sixty out of one hundred was used for the actual trials. This allowed researchers to determine if certain social conditions could reduce the amount of pain someone experienced.

Heterosexual couples were recruited to participate in the study because previous research has found that females are more likely to experience the pain-reducing effects of social connection than males. For this reason, it was always the female participant who was exposed to the thermal stimulation (painful heat). The male partners were then instructed to offer different forms of social support. In some of the trials, the males held their partners' hands. In some of the trials, the males sat next to their partners without any physical touch. In other trials, the males sat in the same room as their partners, but they were separated by a curtain that prevented the couple from being able to see each other. Females rated the amount of pain they experienced after each trial.

The results of the studies demonstrated that pain ratings were highest in the behind-the-curtain condition and lowest in the hand-holding condition. The condition that allowed for eye contact but no physical touch sat in the middle of the other two in terms of reported pain experienced. Interestingly, males also made more accurate guesses about their partners' pain when they were holding their hands rather than when they could make eye contact or were separated by a curtain. What this suggests is that physical touch adds an extra channel of communication by which we can more accurately empathize with and understand one another.

For those of you who want to get really nerdy about what goes on in the brain during these experiments, you are in luck. These particular researchers had the couples wear electroencephalogram (EEG) caps during the entire experiment. EEGs detect electrical impulses in the brain with incredible time sensitivity, so they are particularly useful to investigate when the brain activity between two people is highly coordinated (or synchronized). What they found is that hand-holding during pain administration resulted in greater levels of coordinated alpha brain wave activity between the couples. The more coordinated the alpha waves between two people, the greater the pain-reducing power of hand-holding. In other words, the more synchronized the couple's brains were, the less pain the female experienced. Hand-holding appeared to be useful, at least in part, because it helped promote this neuronal synchrony.

When people are hurting, we cannot always eliminate the source of their pain, but we can reduce how much it hurts. What a relief to know that we do not have to have all the answers or a solution to every problem. If we are willing to simply show up and, if possible, to hold someone's hand, we can create a powerful connection that enhances our ability to empathize with them and reduces the pain that they experience. How life-giving and value-affirming to accept that our mere presence can reduce hurt.

Psych Summary: When someone we love is experiencing pain, our presence can meaningfully reduce the amount of hurt they feel. One of the most powerful ways to do this is through physical touch, like holding your loved one's hand while they experience the pain. When physical touch isn't possible, being visibly present (able to make eye contact during the painful event) can also help to alleviate some of the pain they experience. These simple strategies not only reduce the pain our loved ones experience but also promote a more accurate understanding of their pain. Social neuroscience research shows that hand-holding synchronizes our brain waves with the brain waves of the person in pain. The greater the coordination in this neural activity, the greater the pain-reducing power. Put simply: Hold hands; let it synchronize your brains and reduce your pains.

THINKING THEOLOGICALLY

> Praise be to the God and Father of our Lord Jesus Christ, the Father of compassion and the God of all comfort, who comforts us in all our troubles, so that we can comfort those in any trouble with the comfort we ourselves receive from God. For just as we share abundantly in the sufferings of Christ, so also our comfort abounds through Christ. If we are distressed, it is for your comfort and salvation; if we are comforted, it is for your comfort, which produces in you patient endurance of the same sufferings we suffer. And our hope for you is firm, because we know that just as you share in our sufferings, so also you share in our comfort.
>
> —2 Corinthians 1:3–7 NIV

After addressing his friends in Corinth and introducing himself, Paul names God as one who comforts us in all our troubles, or another way of saying this is that God comforts us when we are in pain or afflicted. Paul goes on to say that they have been suffering a lot, but that the suffering has been matched with comfort from Jesus Christ. In an interesting turn of phrase, he names a kind of mutual suffering and mutual comfort. Paul connects their suffering to the pain that Jesus suffered. Paul writes, "We share abundantly in the sufferings of Christ" (2 Cor. 1:5). But he also writes, "so also our comfort abounds through Christ." There is a sharing of both suffering and comfort (or consolation) in Christ.

Paul then turns this mutuality toward his friends in Corinth. He acknowledges that they "endure the same sufferings that we are also suffering" and that "if we are comforted, it is for your comfort" (2 Cor. 1:6). Without knowing any of the contemporary research, Paul reveals what is true about humanity: We can share suffering and we can share consolation or comfort.

When reading this passage, you might consider that Paul is no stranger to pain. He is out there, being persecuted for the gospel. People were likely verbally harassing him, or putting him in jail, or even beating him, as he writes about elsewhere. Maybe Paul and his traveling companions ran out of money as they traveled and were hungry or sick. This is one way to read the text and evidence from his other writings seem to show that this is likely a faithful way to read the passage. With this context, it seems that there is perhaps a deeper truth about how, as Christians, we are called to share in the suffering and comfort of our neighbors. The message seems to be, "We are in this together. You are not alone—I am here with you."

If we are convinced by Paul's writings and the research from psychology, that we can share pain, how might this insight shift the way we think about loving our neighbor? For psychologist Stephanie Cacioppo, it meant crawling into her husband's hospital bed to be physically with him as he went through cancer treatments for his terminal disease.[2] For you, it might mean holding your child's hand during a dental procedure, maintaining eye contact with someone experiencing pain even when you want to look away, or gathering with friends to sit in silence and weep together when someone's life is impacted by suicide. Sometimes there are genuinely no words. Crying together, holding hands, offering a hug—these physical forms of love offer real consolation, God's real presence to another.

LIVING FAITHFULLY

There are various kinds of pain—physical, psychological, and relational—yet all these forms of pain are registered in a similar area of the brain and can be shared. Below, we consider how you might apply the research we've discussed to various forms of pain when they are experienced by others, but also when you experience them yourself.

When Your Neighbor Is Experiencing Physical or Emotional Pain

Call to mind one person in your life who is experiencing pain. How might you physically be with them, through a hug, sitting in the doctor's office with them, or crawling into their hospital bed, to share in their suffering? If they are too far away to be with physically, could you use a video chat to sit with them virtually in their pain? Reach out and offer to attend an upcoming event with them, not because you have any answers or words of wisdom to alleviate their suffering, but because your presence matters and will help you connect to them and better understand their pain, something that may ultimately help them to feel more seen and less alone.

Physical pain is often (though not always) contained, having a clear beginning and end. Emotional pain on the other hand tends to be harder to predict and often persists beyond the instigating event. So how do we share another person's emotional pain when we cannot necessarily see it or know when it is "over"? Holding someone's hand or giving them a hug in the wake of heartbreak or some particularly difficult news is a great place to start, but it might also be helpful to consider our willingness to listen to someone as they share about their pain.

People are often so afraid of not knowing what to say in response to life's most painful moments that they will avoid a person or a difficult topic altogether. Anyone who has been diagnosed with an illness, struggled with suicidal ideation, or lost a loved one knows the awkward dance of avoiding the hard topic. Take a cancer diagnosis, for example. There is often an initial influx of social support, but it often targets physical (not emotional) needs and fades quickly. Why? Few people are really prepared to sit in the discomfort or awkwardness of a pain that cannot be quickly solved or is unresponsive to "get well" platitudes. Remember the quote we shared in chapter 9 about the importance of listening when having difficult conversations: "Listening is so close to loving that most people don't know the difference." It can guide us here too. As we endeavor to love others better in some of these excruciatingly difficult realities, we do not need to know what to say, we just need to know how to listen.

Brittany experienced the healing power of someone willing to listen in a deeply personal way when she lost her grandfather in September of 2023.

> I was speaking with my counselor, fighting back tears as I shared about the weekend I was in Wyoming for my grandfather's funeral. Seeing the pain in my eyes, she simply asked me, "Can you tell me more about your grandfather, what was he like?" I was a little reluctant (can't you see I am trying not to cry here, lady?), but as I began to share stories about him, I could feel a weight lifting. Through tears and laughter, I was able to share some of my favorite memories. She didn't try to fix it, she didn't try to give me any advice, she didn't try to talk me out of my pain or tell me to think positive—she just sat with me as I waded right into the pain of the loss and also the joy of his memory. My counselor gave me a gift that day. Her curiosity about my grandfather communicated that his life mattered and was worth learning about, even though she never knew him. Her willingness to ask the hard questions and to listen deeply to my response helped to lighten the pain I was experiencing.

This simple act of kindness from a counselor is a strong reminder that one of the worst things we can do is avoid difficult questions and leave others alone as they navigate their most painful moments. We often tell ourselves we do this to avoid making them sad, but more often than not we are actually trying to avoid our own discomfort about what might be said and our inability to know how to respond. We tend to approach the pain of others as if it will go away if we ignore it, or we convince ourselves that we could make it worse by saying the wrong thing. People don't forget their own pain—they just learn to hide it.

The consequence of this avoidance is often a sense of social isolation or burdensomeness for those who are in deep emotional pain. If you have ever experienced tremendous grief, been trapped by depression and suicidal ideation, or been diagnosed with a chronic illness, you know that the associated pain is an all-too-familiar companion. Someone asking you about your experience is unlikely to bring it to mind out of nowhere. It might actually be a relief, giving you permission to stop pretending that it isn't on your mind and giving you some space to be in those thoughts together, rather than all alone.

Is there someone in your life right now who has recently endured a loss or a significantly painful life event? Can you be brave and ask them how they are doing or to share stories of the lost loved one with you?

What if you have someone in your life that you believe is considering suicide. Is it still better to bring it up? Yes. As leading suicide researchers such as Dr. Keyne Law will tell you, bringing it up does not plant the idea in their head.[3] To the contrary, tiptoeing around an issue or concern or ignoring it entirely will often leave someone feeling even more isolated and alone. The very best thing you can do if you are worried someone is contemplating suicide is to ask them directly.[4] It can be as simple as, "I love you, and I'm really worried about you, and I'm wondering if you have been thinking about suicide?" Yes, this is an excruciatingly difficult (and awkward) question to ask, and you need to be prepared for any answer (and know what your next steps will be), but it sends an undeniable signal to the person struggling that their hurt is not invisible, nothing is off-limits to talk about, and they don't have to carry their pain alone.

We all have the opportunity to communicate to others that their lives and their pain matter if we can simply be willing to show up, or ask the real questions—the ones whose answers might make us uncomfortable. If you are lucky enough to be entrusted with someone else's story, you may have no response other than to give them a hug or thank them for sharing. That is okay. Embracing our own discomfort of being unable to identify a solution is an opportunity to remind other people that even in their pain, they are not a problem. As Dr. Kate Bowler, professor of American religious history at Duke Divinity School, reminds us in her life-giving podcast *Everything Happens*, whether you are hurt, heartbroken, or struggling with chronic mental or physical illness, you are not a burden, "you are not the bad thing."

And if someone you know confirms that they are struggling with thoughts of suicide, and especially if they admit they have a plan to do so (a plan is a red alert, emergency-now signal), you might consider helping them get connected to the mental health support they need. Suicide prevention hotlines (call or text 988) are a good place to start if you don't know where else to turn.

When You Are Experiencing Physical or Emotional Pain

There is a temptation to always look outward, to others' pain, but to avoid our own pain, or to self-medicate ourselves away from pain. Please note that we do not mean the occasional ibuprofen for a headache, but we do mean to refer to the increase in alcohol sales that happened during the COVID pandemic, or the way that our college students binge-watch Netflix when they are feeling depressed or isolated. These avoidant behaviors do not remove stress or relieve pain; they simply mask it, and the pain remains in our lives. An alternative to avoiding pain or covering it up is to experience it—to go through it, but to go through it with someone who can carry the pain with us.

Imagine the next thing you have coming up that might involve pain. Are you waiting on test results, caring for a parent with dementia, or getting ready to go into labor? Who might you ask to come hold your hand? If you know you have to visit a doctor and potentially receive bad news, whom might you invite to come with you, so that you can share the stress and burden together rather than alone? How can you give them permission to not have all the answers or to not know what to say to make you feel better and emphasize that it is simply their presence that you know will help to alleviate some of the pain?

When Seasons of Pain Persist

If you or someone you know is in a season of emotional or physical pain, we encourage you to look up Dr. Kate Bowler's blessing, "You are not the bad thing." Replace "you" with your friend or loved one's name, or with your own if you are the one struggling. Use it as a reminder that even in your brokenness, you bear the image of God, and you are a gift to others.

It is awkward and difficult and uncomfortable to move toward people who are in pain, either the social pain of being excluded or physical pain. Our society teaches us to look away, give people privacy, take pain relievers, or just avoid those in pain. Psychological research and theology say we should do just the opposite. We hope that sharing this research reminds you that even when you do not know how to help or cannot change someone's circumstances, your physical presence is a gift to others, and that their presence is a gift to you too.

fourteen

PERSISTING WHEN YOU ARE BEING TREATED POORLY

"But to you who are listening I say: Love your enemies, do good to those who hate you, bless those who curse you, pray for those who mistreat you."

—Luke 6:27–28

LEARNING FROM PSYCHOLOGY

At the heart of loving our neighbors is a requirement to see, to truly behold the image of God in those whom we encounter in our daily lives. This ability to recognize the *imago Dei* in others and to act accordingly is, as we have learned, compromised by several situational factors. Some of these are relatively easy to mitigate (e.g., plan to leave the house earlier to give yourself more time to witness and attend to the pain of those in your path). Other situational factors feel more difficult. Part of this difficulty stems from our own assessments about what can and cannot be controlled.

To our own dismay (and we imagine the dismay of many of you) the thoughts and actions of others fall well outside of the bounds of what we can control. Despite years of fruitless toil, you may still struggle to truly accept that you cannot change the way that someone else thinks, what they believe, or how they behave.

This tends to be a bit unsettling, generally, but in instances when these uncontrollable thoughts or actions are negative and directed at you? Let's just humbly guess (based on our own not-so-great reactions) that love is probably not your knee-jerk response.

While it'd be nice if the wreckage from our rage or righteous indignation was contained within our own egos, the truth is our relationships probably take the biggest hit. We bet that some of the most disastrous relational moments in your life have come in the wake of feeling like someone else thought poorly of you, belittled you, or undermined your self-worth in some way. In short, it is when you feel that someone else is denying the *imago Dei* in you that you are most likely to find yourself gazing back on them as "the opposition" to be crushed or corrected rather than a sibling in Christ.

From a psychological perspective, we can look at this experience through the dynamic lens of dehumanization. While we have talked about dehumanization before, instead of thinking about how we dehumanize others, we can consider what happens when we feel (or know) that we are the ones being dehumanized. Psychologists refer to this process of recognizing that we are *being* dehumanized as "metadehumanization."[1] As we learned in chapter 7, research suggests that there are two primary responses to being on the receiving end of dehumanization. First, in those moments of feeling dehumanized by others, we also begin to dehumanize ourselves. Second, we tend to have a retaliatory response such that we begin to dehumanize those who dehumanize us.

Let's take a closer look at this tendency to deny others humanity when we feel it has first been denied in us. In one set of studies, American participants were provided with fake information about how individuals from other countries perceive Americans in general. In the experimental group, participants were told that individuals from other countries perceive Americans to be substantially "less evolved." Specifically, participants were told that Americans were rated, on average, a 67 out of 100 points on a scale commonly utilized to capture blatant dehumanization.[2] The same people who purportedly rated Americans a 67 rated people from their own country, on average, to be a 96 out of 100 on the same scale. The control group was told that individuals from other countries saw themselves as equally evolved as Americans, ascribing everyone, on average, a 96 out of 100 on the scale.

To ensure participants experienced metadehumanization in the experimental group, the researchers asked a series of follow-up questions about how individuals from other countries perceive Americans (e.g., [People from X country] perceive Americans as a lower form of civilization, less evolved, subhuman). Then, all participants got to share their own opinions about where Americans and people from other countries (including the ones that rated Americans poorly) fall on the 0 to 100 point scale. Results from these studies demonstrated that individuals in the experimental conditions who had been told Americans were perceived as less evolved were more likely to dehumanize people from other countries in return. This is the experimental equivalent to the sizzling playground retort, "No I'm not, you are!"

Additional studies by the same authors demonstrated that the tendency to dehumanize others after being dehumanized bled into more extreme attitudes, like an increased willingness to support the torture of individuals who belonged to the other group. The basic principle here is something we are all probably familiar with on some level: When others belittle or harm us, our initial reaction is to belittle and harm them in return. What is so interesting about this set of studies is that it reveals how subtle this process can be. We might think that our assessment of another person's (or people group's) humanity is grounded in a theological understanding of God as Creator who imbued every person with his image. While you may believe that, as we do, this reason, grounded in Scripture, is unlikely to buffer us from the tendency to abandon that image that we are all God's children once we've had our own humanity denied. This research provides sobering evidence that our attitudes about and treatment toward others is readily malleable in response to how we are told those people see or perceive us. If this is true when strangers rate us on a scale, the backlash from more direct and personal forms of dehumanization are likely to be even more significant.

Psych Summary: Being on the receiving end of dehumanization—feeling like our thoughts, needs, or abilities are being underestimated or undervalued—activates a chain of often nonconscious reactions. First, we can start to dehumanize ourselves, thinking less of or undervaluing our own humanity. Second, we tend to retaliate by dehumanizing those who dehumanize us. This cycle of dehumanization is in direct opposition to our goal to love our neighbors as ourselves because it affects both how we view our neighbors and how we view ourselves. Disrupting this cycle of dehumanization starts with recognizing it exists and being intentional about affirming our own humanity and the humanity of others when we feel we are being denied core aspects of our humanity.

THINKING THEOLOGICALLY

> But the people were thirsty for water there, and they grumbled against Moses. They said, "Why did you bring us up out of Egypt to make us and our children and livestock die of thirst?" Then Moses cried out to the LORD, "What am I to do with these people? They are almost ready to stone me." The LORD answered Moses, "Go out in front of the people. Take with you some of the elders of Israel and take in your hand the staff with which you struck the Nile, and go. I will stand there before you by the rock at Horeb. Strike the rock, and water will come out of it for the people to drink." So Moses did this in the sight of the elders of Israel.
>
> —Exodus 17:3–6

Dominique Gilliard gave a powerful keynote speech about our call as Christians to love others well at a faith formation conference for those in ministry.[3] He spoke passionately about the perils of dehumanization and the biblical mandate to care for the sick, the poor, and the hurting. And in it he shared a little-known story about Martin Luther King Jr. as a child. As the story goes, prior to starting kindergarten Martin Luther King Jr.'s best friend in the neighborhood was White. Schools had been desegregated, which meant that the two friends would both be attending the same school. Shortly after the school year began, the White boy visited Martin to share with him that he could no longer be his friend because he was Black.

Upon hearing this, Martin's parents sat down to help him process what had just happened. Mr. and Mrs. King's response in that moment was nothing short of profound. They told Martin to never forget that he is somebody, that he matters. They affirmed his identity and condemned any act, including the friend's, grounded in racist ideologies that served to undermine his sense of self-worth or value as a child of God. But they did not stop there. They also told him to remember that his friend, who just broke his heart and denied him his value as a human because of his skin color, was also somebody who matters. In essence, the Kings said, Martin, you are created in the image of God; you matter. Don't ever let anyone take that away from you. Also know that your friend who just hurt you, he is also created in the image of God; he also matters. Don't ever try to take that away from him. Let us be clear, this does not condone the discrimination. It does serve as a reminder that even when it is distorted by ungodly and unjust actions, every person bears God's image and is loved unconditionally.

As White women born and raised in the United States, we will never truly know or understand the pain and suffering that Black Americans have faced and continue to face in this country as a result of racist ideologies and the compounding effects of exclusionary laws and social norms. We have so much to learn from the Kings and the grace, wisdom, love, and strength they had in that moment (and countless others). A moment when their own identities as Black Americans were being devalued. A moment when they were witnessing the emotional anguish of their son as he navigated blatant racism and discrimination, not just from anyone, but from someone he loved and trusted. A moment when it would have been easy to be overtaken by the instinct to dehumanize in response to being dehumanized. And yet, they chose love. They chose to uphold the *imago Dei*, not just for their son but also for the child who hurt him.

Throughout the Bible we also see many examples of people who respond to hate or dehumanization with love, compassion, and humanizing behavior. The story of Jacob and Esau is one example. After Esau's blessing was stolen by his younger brother Jacob, Esau was angry and vowed to kill Jacob. Years later when Jacob returned, instead of attacking him, Esau ran to Jacob and embraced him with love. Curiously, we don't see in the story what changed in Esau. Maybe a lesson here is that time can also help us to approach people who have harmed us more lovingly.

Another example is the one of Moses quoted at the beginning of this chapter. Moses was often on the receiving end of criticism from the very people he led out of oppression. After fleeing slavery in Egypt, the Israelites wandered around in the desert, thirsty, tired, and angry. The laments of the Israelites were often, ironically, directed toward Moses even though he was their liberator. This is evident in the rhetoric of the Israelites who accuse Moses of bringing them out into the desert to die of thirst. Moses, who was presumably also thirsty, probably wanted to begin hurling insults of his own, or rebuking the Israelites for being ungrateful.

At least in this instance, however, he refrains from such behaviors, and instead Moses cries out to God. His prayer, while short, is powerful because it disrupts a cycle of criticism, blame, and dehumanization. It is also clear from the short prayer that Moses sees these people as children of God, who bear God's image and are in God's care. Moses beholds their value and dignity, recognizes his own limitations, and turns to God for guidance and tangible next steps to care for the Israelites well and attend to their needs. Even though tensions have been building for days, this is not the first criticism Moses has received. The prayer Moses speaks to God is a pause, one that allows Moses to disrupt a potentially escalating cycle of negativity with a response that is full of grace and love.

LIVING FAITHFULLY

In a section of *Church Dogmatics* on what it means to be human, titled "Theological Anthropology," theologian Karl Barth claims that we live into our true, God-given, full humanity through our relationships with other people.[4] According to Barth, mutuality is critical to these relationships, specifically through mutual seeing, mutual hearing, and mutual serving in the context of delight. Living out this type of relationship involves beautiful interdependence, vulnerability, and joy. It is not insignificant that he wrote in Germany during World War II, where he was seeing firsthand how a failure to see, hear, serve, and enjoy people led to tragic social divisions and ultimately the death of millions of Jews.

The idea of mutuality in relationships is as powerful at the national level as it is in our everyday relationships. Yet, this is really hard, perhaps even impossible to actually live out, although that doesn't mean we shouldn't try. Even if you want to live in this way with the people you know, there is no guarantee they will do the same. At times clear power dynamics are at play (e.g., boss and employee, professor and student) that can thwart our ability to come to a relationship in a truly mutual way. In other (worst-case) scenarios, people might be actively trying to undermine us, hurt our feelings, get us fired, or, in extreme circumstances, cause us physical harm. Like Moses, we might wonder what we are supposed to do when people are insulting us and hurling rocks at us.

The reflex to pick up a stone and return the dehumanizing words aimed at us sounds viciously satisfying; however, it is the furthest thing from love. So, what do we do instead? How do we respond when others think about or treat us poorly? How should we respond when we are on the receiving end of unjust beliefs and actions? Is it even possible to get to a place like Moses, where our immediate reaction is to turn to God rather than to retaliate with ridicule or disdain?

Psychological research is helpful here, explaining how our knee-jerk responses are not only common but often outside of our conscious awareness. We are not aware of the significant changes in the way we interpret life when we are being dehumanized. To the contrary, people tend to evaluate their success at loving their enemies in terms of a lack of direct outward harm. For example, you might congratulate yourself, thinking, I didn't retaliate by yelling at them. But such "successes" do not get to the heart of the issue.

Negative encounters like these, that are aimed at us, compromise the value and dignity that we perceive in the other person. Hear us on this: even if you manage to regulate yourself enough to not respond hurtfully in an outward or obvious manner, there is likely a change going on inward that denies that person a piece of their humanity and predisposes you to act more hurtfully, or at least less kindly, in future encounters. A shorthand way of explaining this is that once you've been hurt, you are less likely to see and treat the person who hurt you as fully human. This can breed contempt (remember chapter 7?).

Just knowing we are vulnerable to these shifts in attitude toward others can help us buffer ourselves from these effects. When you feel the snarl of rage as you begin to compose the perfect comeback, you can take a deep breath and remember that when we feel dehumanized, our instinct is to retaliate. You might then think of Moses and move from retaliation to curiosity by asking God, "What am I to do with these people?" You could even soften your rage by adding details about their situation, "What am I to do with these people who have followed me into the desert, who are hungry, who are homesick?"

We can choose to show up with love and kindness even when we are met with dehumanizing perceptions from others that are beyond our control. Knowing that you will automatically tend to dehumanize those who dehumanize you can help you to see it when it is happening and to prepare to intentionally counter it. Eugene Peterson's translation of Luke 6:27–28 in *The Message* says, "Love your enemies, let them bring out the best in you. Not the worst." So how exactly can we prepare to increase the odds that the actions or attitudes of others don't bring out the worst in us, but rather the best?

The instructions in Luke 6 to pray for our enemies offers one fruitful approach. The power of turning to God in prayer, as well as a template for that prayer, is beautifully depicted in the story of Moses, who immediately turns to God. Careful attention to Moses's prayer suggests that it is not as simple as "giving them to God" or praying for them in a way that assumes prayer is the only action. Moses's prayer specifically says, "What am I to *do*?" Like Moses, maybe an action-oriented prayer is a way for us to disrupt the cycle of dehumanization.

Let's practice it now.

Consider a time when someone made you feel subhuman, like you were not as smart, not as important, not as valuable. . . . We have been thinking a lot about how this happens in even very subtle ways, like someone calling another person "childish" as an insult, as well as big ways, like someone spitting a sexist or racist slur in your direction. Take a moment to write about that experience of being treated as "less than" and how it made you feel.

Now, take this moment to pause and lift that person to God in the prayer. Modeling your prayer after Moses's, asking God what to *do*, to reveal ways that you can love this person, affirming their dignity, and acting in ways that will help you care for or meet their needs.

A second way to be prepared might be to have a simple saying or a phrase, like Martin Luther King Jr.'s parents—You are somebody; they are somebody too. The more these ideas are explicitly expressed in your own life, even when you aren't feeling dehumanized, the easier they are to fall back on when the pain of being dehumanized begins to set in. A few years ago, Brittany's sister gifted her a children's book called *Everybody Is Somebody*. The last page reads, "Everybody is somebody, we need to love all."[5] We can't help but wonder now if the author knew of the story of Martin Luther King Jr. and how his parents responded. You don't need to have kids to benefit from having a clear and concise reminder about your own value and the value of others. Here, we will remind you.

> You are a precious child of God, created in his image, and loved beyond comprehension. The person who made you feel like you were not worthy, the one who insulted you—God loves them too. They are also a precious child of God and also infinitely loved. Today, ask God to give you the tenderness to see the belovedness of everyone you encounter and to be affirmed in your own identity as a deeply loved child of God.

CONCLUSION: BEING WHO GOD MADE YOU TO BE

Based on what we read in the Bible, God wants us to stretch beyond our comfort zones, but he is not calling us to be someone else entirely. This is true of Moses, Joseph, Sarah, Hagar, Ruth, Paul, Mary Magdalene, and almost every biblical figure you can think of. The theological term for this stretching is *sanctification*. We are created good and loved and accepted and adopted by God, just the way we are (even though sin distorts everything to make us fail to recognize this and fully live into this). It is also true that we are called to be open to how the Holy Spirit is making us more loving, more like Jesus. The way this happens in real life is that we can both embrace what makes us unique and also be looking for ways God might be changing or teaching us. One example of this is that there are ways to love others as an introvert and as an extrovert. The people we read about in the Bible include the full spectrum of humanity. While it might be tempting to compare ourselves to one another, the truth is that each person is one of a kind, with different gifts. And each of us adds uniquely valuable skills and perspectives to the body of Christ.

In psychology, we capture this with an equation that looks at the interaction between someone's personality and their environment. We refer to this as the *person x situation fit*. The basic principle of this concept is to acknowledge that, depending on our personalities, we will thrive in different environments, benefit from different types of interventions, and rely on others to supplement our weaknesses and blind spots. We do not expect that all the concepts in this book resonate with you all equally, or even that you are all being called to live faithfully and love your neighbors in the exact same ways. While we hope this book challenged you and pushed you out of your comfort zone, we are not suggesting you be someone you are not.

Take personality, for example. Katie is a ten out of ten on the extroversion scale. When she first moved to Seattle, she collected the phone numbers of other moms at the playground like someone looking for a date in the '80s. Brittany is considerably more introverted, meaning that she tends to be depleted rather than energized by social interactions. Taking the person x situation fit approach suggests that it might look different for each of us to love our neighbor.

If you are more on the introverted side, loving well might look like paying attention to the tiny details, noticing when someone feels left out or seems "off" in a group interaction and following up with them one-on-one to check in. If you are more extroverted, it might mean utilizing that aggressive friendliness to recruit people to the *Harry Potter*–themed inflatable hot tub party you are hosting: something that brings everyone together in the first place.

Having different strengths is also one of the reasons why community is so important and it takes a village to love others well. On the night of Brittany's wedding, we combined our personal superpowers to make sure that one of the guests, who had recently had a relationship end, felt well-loved and included. Brittany, seeing the need and empathizing with what it would feel like to be at a celebration of love shortly after your relationship ended, asked Katie to be this guest's unofficial date. Katie delivered with her own superpowers of friendliness and fun. While we did not ask this friend how the night went, we are pretty sure, based on her dancing, laughing, and heartfelt conversations, that the wedding was not a night when she was left alone in the pain of an ended relationship, but felt cared for and listened to in all the (potential) awkwardness of attending a wedding without a plus-one.

One of the reasons we make a great team is because we are different and our differences complement one another. Katie is great at making people feel seen and loved by including them in a group event, while Brittany is good at making people feel loved by noticing small but significant details that help them feel known.

What about you? What is your natural superpower? How do you most readily make people feel loved? How can you lean into and amplify that aspect of yourself while also challenging yourself to stretch outside of your comfort zone at times? How can you surround yourself with other people who will help you see the value in showing up to love in ways that might come less naturally to you? We suspect, as has been the case for us, that being with these people will inspire you to love in ways that are new for you too.

Each of us has a different neighborhood map where we encounter different people. We are placed in different locations so we can bring the Spirit's loving presence to the weddings, elevators, offices, classrooms, hallways, parking garages, airports, inflatable hot tubs, and waiting rooms where we encounter our neighbors. Loving our neighbor includes seeing our own role in bringing love, empathy, and compassion into these spaces and encounters. We hope you find ways to tailor these challenges so that they stay fresh and authentic to you, while still pushing you outside of your normal everyday routine. Get out there, love better. We will be awkwardly, aggressively, and earnestly attempting to do the same.

FINAL NOTE FROM THE AUTHORS

What a journey it is to try to love our neighbors better! As we wrote this book and began receiving feedback from beloved colleagues, family, and friends, we began to realize just how complex and dynamic it is to unpack all the thoughts, emotions, and situations that get in the way of loving our neighbors. There is so much more we could say about parenting better, growing and developing one's character, digging more deeply into justice, and learning and unlearning how to love others well from our own location as two White women who have spent so much time living, teaching, and parenting in Seattle, all through the lens of theology and psychology. We look forward to continuing with you on this faithful journey of growth as we take small but significant steps in becoming more like Jesus and help each other out as we make mistakes along the way. If you'd like to follow along, you can join us on Substack at lovingbetter.substack.com. We hope to see you there!

GLOSSARY

animalistic dehumanization A belief (implicit or explicit) that another person or people group is less evolved or more animalistic than yourself or a group with which you identify. Animalistic dehumanization often takes the shape of denying other humans' high-level cognitive traits that are believed to distinguish humans from nonhuman animals, but can also be evidenced in using animalistic language or language that implies less sophistication or civilization when referring to other people or groups. (See N. Haslam and S. Loughnan, "Dehumanization and Infrahumanization," *Annual Review of Psychology* 65 [2014]: 399–423, doi: 10.1146/annurev-psych-010213-115045.)

attribution theory A social psychological framework describing the human tendency to speculate about the causes of another's actions or behaviors. In other words, humans often ask the question, Why did they do that? Answers tend to fall in line with either situational explanations or dispositional explanations (see **dispositional attribution** and **situational attribution** below).

belief perseverance The tendency for an already held belief to persist even in the face of counter information. (See Ziva Kunda, "The Case for Motivated Reasoning," *Psychological Bulletin* 108, no. 3 (1990): 480.)

blaming the victim The tendency to blame people for their victimization or unfair treatment, typically motivated (nonconsciously) by a desire to see the world as a fair place. (See William Ryan, *Blaming the Victim* [Vintage, 1976].)

bystander effect A phenomenon whereby the more people who witness an emergency, the less likely any one of them is to help. (See J. M. Darley and B. Latane, "Bystander Intervention in Emergencies: Diffusion of Responsibility," *Journal of Personality and Social Psychology* [1968]: 377–83.)

cognitive overload The phenomenon whereby human working memory capacity is maxed out and can no longer effectively process new information. The theory, initially applied to learning, has been extended to decision-making and other cognitive processes that are similarly harmed when trying to process too much information at one time. (See J. Sweller, "Cognitive Load During Problem Solving: Effects on Learning," *Cognitive Science* 12 [1988]: 257–85.)

confirmation bias Systematic tendency to seek out, notice, and remember information that is consistent with already held beliefs. Information that is inconsistent with pre-established beliefs is therefore less likely to be sought out, more likely to be overlooked when available, and less likely to be remembered. (See J. Klayman, "Varieties of Confirmation Bias," *Psychology of Learning and Motivation* 32 [1995]: 385–418.)

contact hypothesis Social psychological framework that describes intergroup contact (interactions between two different groups) as a primary mechanism to reduce prejudice or animosity between groups. The contact hypothesis identifies several criteria for intergroup contact to be most effective at improving intergroup attitudes. These criteria include (1) interdependence, (2) common goal, (3) equal status, (4) friendly or neutral environment for interaction, (5) interactions with multiple group members, and (6) social support or norms that uphold equity for each group. (See Gordon Allport, *The Nature of Prejudice* [Doubleday, 1954].)

contempt A social emotion characterized by an implicit or explicit sense of one's own superiority relative to another person or people group. This superiority manifests in looking down on another person or people group, often with a sense of pity, disgust, or irritation that signals another person is "less than."

cultural humility A concept that extends awareness, openness, and "egolessness" about the limits of one's own knowledge to the norms, experiences, and customs of another person or people group. Cultural humility is displayed through curiosity about and respect for ways of speaking, living, believing, and thinking that differ from your own. (For a recent theory paper on cultural humility see Cynthia Foronda, "A Theory of Cultural Humility," *Journal of Transcultural Nursing* 31 [2020]: 7–12.)

diffusion of responsibility A phenomenon whereby a person's sense of responsibility to act in a prosocial way decreases the more individuals are present. As such, a diffusion of responsibility (feeling less responsible) is often cited as a primary reason why the **bystander effect** occurs. (See J. M. Darley and B. Latane, "Bystander Intervention in Emergencies: Diffusion of Responsibility," *Journal of Personality and Social Psychology* [1968]: 377–83.)

dispositional attribution The perception or belief that a particular behavior is caused by personality traits or internal characteristics.

egocentrism Tendency to be grounded in and biased by our own experiences of the world, making it difficult to understand another person's experience or perspective fully.

empathic accuracy A term used by researchers to quantify how accurately people are able to perceive the emotions of other individuals.

empathy-altruism hypothesis A framework to predict when people are most likely to help that centers empathy as the core prerequisite for helping to occur. (See C. Daniel Batson, David A. Lishner, and Eric L. Stocks, "The Empathy-Altruism Hypothesis," *The Oxford Handbook of Prosocial Behavior* [2015]: 259–81.)

enacted space A theological term used when discussing the physical design of neighborhoods and cities which either allow for space to be inhabited and connections to form, or for distance to be created between people. (See Eric O. Jacobsen, *The Space Between: A Christian Engagement with the Built Environment* [Baker Academic, 2012].)

fundamental attribution error A systematic tendency to overweight dispositional and underweight situational attributions when trying to understand another person's negative behaviors relative to our own. For example, they cut me off in traffic because they are a jerk (dispositional). I cut them off in traffic because I was distracted by my toddler throwing a ball at me while I'm driving (situational). (See L. Ross, "The Intuitive Psychologist and His Shortcomings: Distortions in the Attribution Process," in *Advances in Experimental Social Psychology*, ed. L. Berkowitz, vol. 10 [Academic Press, 1977].)

hindsight bias A systematic cognitive error whereby people assume that the outcome of an event was more obvious, inevitable, or predictable than it actually was before the results were known. Sometimes this is summarized as a feeling that one "knew it all along." It is also well captured by the colloquialism "hindsight is 20/20." Hindsight bias was first described by Baruch Fischhoff in 1975. An impressive review of 818 papers investigating the hindsight bias was written by Neal Roese and Kathleen Vohs in 2012. (See Baruch Fischhoff, "Hindsight Is Not Equal to Foresight: The Effect of Outcome Knowledge on Judgment Under Uncertainty," *Journal of Experimental Psychology: Human Perception and Performance* 1 [1975]: 288–99; Neal J. Roese and Kathleen D. Vohs, "Hindsight Bias," *Perspectives on Psychological Science* 7, no. 5 [2012]: 411–26, https://doi.org/10.1177/1745691612454303.)

in-group Social psychological term used to describe groups with which we personally identify. The term is thus relative and who or what counts as an in-group varies from person to person.

interpersonal interactions A general term in social psychology that refers to an interaction between two people. *Inter* (between) is in contrast to *intra* (within). Thus, interpersonal consequences are consequences that impact the dynamics between people, whereas intrapersonal consequences are those that affect the dynamics within a person.

iPhone effect The phenomenon whereby the mere presence of an electronic device (such as an iPhone) negatively affects interpersonal interactions. These consequences are likely driven by the fact that electronic devices automatically recruit cognitive resources (i.e., some level of attention) to monitor them given they may "go off" at any point in time. (See S. Misra, L. Cheng, J. Genevie, and M. Yuan, "The iPhone Effect: The Quality of In Person Social Interactions in the Presence of Mobile Devices," *Environment and Behavior* 48 [2014]: 275–98, https://doi.org/10.1177/0013916514539755.)

just-world phenomenon An (often nonconscious) belief that the world is just and thus good things happen to good people—or people who make good choices—and bad things happen to bad people—or people who make bad choices. This belief operates to preserve our own sense of safety and control by insisting that if we are careful to control our own behaviors, we can avoid bad or unjust things happening to us. (See M. J. Lerner, "The Desire for Justice and Reactions to Victims," in *Altruism and Helping Behavior*, ed. J. Macaulay and L. Berkowitz [Academic Press, 1970].)

mechanistic dehumanization A belief (implicit or explicit) that another person or people group is more robotic or machine-like than yourself or a group with which you identify. Mechanistic dehumanization often takes the shape of denying other humans' emotional depth or traits (e.g., caring, thoughtful) that are believed to distinguish humans from machines. (See N. Haslam and S. Loughnan, "Dehumanization and Infrahumanization," *Annual Review of Psychology* 65 [2014]: 399–423, doi: 10.1146/annurev-psych-010213-115045.)

mere exposure effect A psychological phenomenon that describes how repeated exposure to a stimulus (like a person or a product) increases liking for the stimulus.

metadehumanization The process of knowing or recognizing that we are being dehumanized by another person or people group. (See N. Kteily, G. Hodson, and E. Bruneau, "They See Us as Less Than Human: Metadehumanization Predicts Intergroup Conflict via Reciprocal Dehumanization," *Journal of Personality and Social Psychology* 110 (2016): 343–70, https://doi.org/10.1037/pspa0000044.)

out-group Social psychological term used to describe groups with which we do not personally identify. The term is thus relative and who or what counts as an out-group varies from person to person.

paradox of generosity A phenomenon whereby people experience positive personal consequences (e.g., well-being, happiness, purpose) when they purposefully give their resources (e.g., time and money) to those in need. (See Chris Smith and Hilary Davidson, *The Paradox of Generosity* [Oxford University Press, 2014].)

person x situation fit A framework that emphasizes the importance of establishing alignment between personality types and environmental or situational factors. In essence, it recognizes that not every person is going to thrive in every environment or benefit from the same strategies to change behavior.

planning fallacy A systematic tendency to believe that projects and activities will unfold as expected and in a shorter period of time than is reasonable based on past experiences with similar projects that have been marked by complications and take longer than anticipated to complete. (See Daniel Kahneman and Amos Tversky, "Intuitive Prediction: Biases and Corrective Procedures," *TIMS Studies in Management Science* 12 [1979]: 313–27.)

pluralistic ignorance The misconception that others are interpreting an event in a certain way (e.g., often as if it is not an emergency), when they are actually not (e.g., internally they are also panicked or simply have not yet noticed what you are currently noticing). (See B. Latane and J. M. Darley, *The Unresponsive Bystander: Why Doesn't He Help?* [Appleton-Century-Crofts, 1970].)

prejudice Any negative evaluation of a person or people group due simply to their association with a particular group. Prejudice makes an assumption that all people who share one particular feature (e.g., skin color, age) are all the same on another feature (e.g., work ethic, morality).

propinquity effect A phenomenon in social psychology that describes the importance of "functional distance" between people for determining when relationships are likely to form. Highly functional areas, those that receive a high level of human foot traffic (e.g., staircases and mail rooms), create opportunities for interpersonal interactions that are likely to generate relationships. Thus, when people are located closer to these highly functional areas, they are more likely to be well connected to people located at farther physical distances because they are at a heightened likelihood of "bumping into" people who live or are located farther away. (See Leon Festinger, Stanley Schachter, and Kurt Back, "The Spatial Ecology of Group Formation," in *Social Pressures in Informal Groups: A Study of Human Factors in Housing*, ed. Leon Festinger, Stanley Schachter, and Kurt Back [Harper, 1950], 33–59.)

prosocial behavior A general term in social psychology that refers to any action that is intended to benefit another person. Prosocial behavior is distinct from altruism, because altruism requires a desire to help even if there is a cost to the self. Prosocial behavior does not necessarily have to come at a cost. Thus, all altruism is prosocial behavior, but not all prosocial behavior is altruism.

providence *Providence* is the word used to discuss God's relationship to world events. Some positions believe that everything is known and planned by God ahead of time, while other positions believe that humanity is truly free and the future is open even as God is actively present with us in the world. There are biblical passages that you can cite to support both positions. The significance of the idea of providence, regardless of the position you hold, is that God loves and saves the world, bringing life out of death. And also that God is *with* humanity and *for* humanity, not as a distant deity but as Jesus Christ, who knows what it is like to be a human.

proximity A general term in the social psychology literature that simply refers to the physical distance between two people.

relative deprivation A sense that you have less than or are worse off than another person or group that is grounded in selective (whether conscious or nonconscious) comparisons to people that have more than you. This phenomenon is situated in the broader relative deprivation theory that emphasizes the reference points we use for social comparison and can apply to a wide array of topics (e.g., wealth, happiness, opportunities) and consequences. (See Simone I. Flynn, "Relative Deprivation Theory," *Theories of Social Movements: Sociology Reference Guide* [2011]: 100–110.)

residential mobility A term describing geographic movement from place to place. Such movement is often directly associated with shifting social groups and interpersonal connections.

residential stability A term describing geographic consistency in place. Such consistency is often directly associated with more stable social groups and interpersonal connections.

sanctification A general term used in theology that means being made holy. Different traditions explain how this happens in different ways. Theologians generally agree that sanctification is the process by which the Holy Spirit makes us more like Jesus. This means moving away from sin and toward being the person God made us to be.

situational attribution The perception or belief that a particular behavior is caused by situational or circumstantial factors.

social exchange theory A framework to predict when people are most likely to help that centers a cost benefit analysis that ultimately favors one's self as the core prerequisite for helping to occur. (For recent review see Rehan Ahmad, Muhammad Rafay Nawaz, Muhammad Ishtiaq Ishaq, Mumtaz Muhammad Khan, and Hafiz Ahmad Ashraf, "Social Exchange Theory: Systematic Review and Future Directions," *Frontiers in Psychology* 13 [2023]: 1015921.)

stages of helping Psychologists define five requirements that often need to be met in order for someone to engage in a prosocial action. These include noticing the event, accurately recognizing the event as an emergency or one in which help is necessary, assuming responsibility to meet the assessed need, having a sense of competence or knowledge about how one could help or meet the need, and finally, determining that the costs of helping are relatively minimal. (See B. Latane and J. M. Darley, *The Unresponsive Bystander: Why Doesn't He Help?* [Appleton-Century-Crofts, 1970].)

stereotype content model Social psychological framework that describes two primary dimensions of person perception: warmth and competence. (See A. J. Cuddy, S. T. Fiske, and P. Glick, "Warmth and Competence as Universal Dimensions of Social Perception: The Stereotype Content Model and the BIAS Map," *Advances in Experimental Social Psychology* 40 [2008]: 61–149.)

supererogation *Supererogation* is used to refer to moments when we go beyond what duty requires of us. Theologically, the call to love our neighbor can demand more of us than we are capable of offering and yet, sometimes, we still answer that call. (See Eric Gregory, "Supererogation for Protestants?," in *The Ethics of Grace: Engaging Gerald McKenny*, ed. Michael Mawson and Paul Martens [New York: Bloomsbury, 2023], 53–68.)

theory of mind The awareness that other minds are distinct from one's own, containing their own thoughts, feelings, beliefs, and experiences.

tragedy of the commons A term coined by ecologist Garrett Hardin to describe the depletion of a shared (often renewable) resource because of overuse by individuals acting out of their own self-interest. (See Garrett Hardin, "The Tragedy of the Commons," in

Classic Papers in Natural Resource Economics Revisited [Routledge, 2018], 145–56.)

zero sum game A situation (or belief) where one person's gain is directly and equally related to another person's loss and vice versa, which often creates a sense of direct competition.

ACKNOWLEDGMENTS

Our collective and heartfelt thanks go out to so many folks who have offered invaluable forms of support along our individual and shared journeys. To all those we have listed and any we may have unintentionally missed, thank you for the part you have played in our work and in our lives.

Thank you to our *students* who participated in our experiments and took our class on Neighbor Love. You were there for our early and awkward attempts to work together across disciplines and taught us so much through your insightful questions and passions for loving all people better. A special shout-out to Caitlin Thomas, Lucy Israel, Laura Shigeta, Kate Underwood, Rebecca Hodges, Bella Rivera, Isabelle Dennis, Anna Wiedemann (Dischinger), Jamie Lee, Mary Capili (Charleson), and Leah Fingerhut, who assisted in research that helped inform chapters in this book. We are so lucky to have had the chance to learn alongside all of you.

Our gratitude to our *colleagues*, and especially Drs. Katy Tangenberg, Baine Craft, and Brian Lugioyo, who encouraged us to work together and supported our interdisciplinary ideas in ways that allowed us to break traditional academic silos. We are also deeply grateful to Dr. Paul Youngbin Kim and Rev. Dominique Dubois Gilliard, who shared their time and expertise with us, providing thoughtful and edifying feedback for this book. We have loved working with Chloe Guillot, who turned our napkin sketches into clear maps and images for the book.

Thank you to the *generous donors* who have funded our scholarship and created opportunities for us to imagine interdisciplinary projects. Thank you to the Theological Integration Fellowship program at Seattle Pacific University that allowed Brittany to complete seminary classes, and all her seminary professors (including Katie!), who graciously let her write some of these book chapters in place of traditional papers. We are grateful to John Perry, Joanna Leidenhag, and Sarah Lane Ritchie, who hosted us as fellows at the New Visions in Theological Anthropology (NViTA) Initiative at St. Andrews University, generously funded by the John Templeton Foundation. Our thanks to Jennifer Rothschild, Michael Lamb, and the Educating Character Initiative team at Wake Forest University, as well as the Lilly Endowment, Inc., whose support has allowed us to amplify work that enhances virtues like neighbor love in our college classrooms and beyond.

Thank you to our *editors* at Eerdmans, who offered constructive feedback that made our ideas clearer and helped us grow as authors, and to our *agents* Laura Bardolph and David Bratt, who were the first to see the potential for this book and believed it was worth printing and sharing with the world.

We are grateful to all our *family and friends* for loving and encouraging us through so many seasons of life and to Ulla Tausen, Bill and Dorothy Lewis, and Gay Koenemann, who enthusiastically volunteered to read the earliest (and roughest) forms of this project.

Thank you to our *partners*, John and Kris, who lovingly support our ambitious agendas, travel plans, and scholarly pursuits. Thank you for the sacrifices you have made to help this dream of ours come true. And to our wonderfully rambunctious and oh so lovable kids, George, Paul, Will, Odyn, and Aksel: thank you for being you and for entertaining yourselves (aka making Rice Crispy treats and sneaking shows) while we wrote and worked together. We love you big-time, and every day—even when we get it wrong—we are, and will always be, trying to love you better.

NOTES

CHAPTER ONE

1. Answer to quiz question #5.

2. Answer to quiz question #7.

3. Scripture quotations in this book are from the New Revised Standard Version (NRSV) unless otherwise noted.

4. Jay Pathak and Dave Runyon, *The Art of Neighboring* (Baker, 2012).

5. Brenda Salter McNeil, "Learning to Love Your Neighbor," sermon preached at Quest Church, Seattle, WA, July 9, 2023, https://tinyurl.com/mpw8sw4.

CHAPTER TWO

1. Answer to quiz question #4.

2. J. M. Darley and C. D. Batson, "'From Jerusalem to Jericho': A Study of Situational and Dispositional Variables in Helping Behavior," *Journal of Personality and Social Psychology* 27 (1973): 100–108.

3. Simone Weil, *Waiting for God* (Harper Collins, 2009), 64.

4. J. de la Fuente, J. Santiago, A. Román, C. Dumitrache, and D. Casasanto, "When You Think About It, Your Past Is in Front of You: How Culture Shapes Spatial Conceptions of Time," *Psychological Science* 25, no. 9 (2014): 1682–90, https://doi.org/10.1177/0956797614534695.

5. M. D. Hills, "Kluckhohn and Strodtbeck's values orientation theory," *Online Readings in Psychology and Culture* 4, no. 4 (2002): 3.

6. Leah Bouterse and Cara Wall-Scheffler, "Children Are Not Like

Other Loads: A Cross-Cultural Perspective on the Influence of Burdens and Companionship on Human Walking," *PeerJ* 6:e5547 (2018): https://doi.org/10.7717/peerj.5547.

CHAPTER THREE

1. Answer to quiz question #9.

2. L. Bickman, A. Teger, T. Gabriele, C. McLaughlin, M. Berger, and E. Sunaday, "Dormitory Density and Helping Behavior," *Environment and Behavior* 5, no. 4 (1973): 465–90, https://doi.org/10.1177/001391657300500406.

3. Global Mind Project, "Age of First Smartphone/Tablet and Mental Wellbeing Outcomes," Sapien Labs, May 15, 2023, https://tinyurl.com/m654mf6y.

4. A. K. Przybylski and N. Weinstein, "Can You Connect with Me Now? How the Presence of Mobile Communication Technology Influences Face-to-Face Conversation Quality," *Journal of Social and Personal Relationships* 30 (2013): 237–46.

5. S. Misra, L. Cheng, J. Genevie, and M. Yuan, "The iPhone Effect: The Quality of In-Person Social Interactions in the Presence of Mobile Devices," *Environment and Behavior* 48 (2014): 275–98, https://doi.org/10.1177/0013916514539755.

6. Misra et al., "iPhone Effect."

7. Glennon Doyle, "There's No Such Thing as Other People's Children," *Momastery*, February 9, 2016, https://tinyurl.com/3kfjnnn4.

8. Jenny Odell, *How to Do Nothing: Resisting the Attention Economy* (Melville House, 2020).

CHAPTER FOUR

1. Answer to quiz question #2.

2. See Channel Miller, *Know My Name: A Memoir* (Penguin Books, 2019).

CHAPTER FIVE

1. R. Janoff-Bulman, C. Timko, and L. L. Carli, "Cognitive Biases in

Blaming the Victim," *Journal of Experimental Social Psychology* 21, no. 2 (1985): 161–77.

2. P. Y. Kim, *Culture and Psychology in a Christian Perspective* (Baker Academic, forthcoming).

3. D. W. Sue, "Eliminating Cultural Oppression in Counseling: Toward a General Theory," *Journal of Counseling Psychology* 25, no. 5 (1978): 419.

4. Dietrich Bonhoeffer, *No Rusty Swords,* ed. Edwin H. Robertson (Harper & Row, 1965), 22.

CHAPTER SIX

1. These protections came through the Equal Credit Opportunity Act passed in 1974. See https://tinyurl.com/mvrhjmjy.

2. Amy J. C. Cuddy, Susan T. Fiske, and Peter Glick, "Warmth and Competence as Universal Dimensions of Social Perception: The Stereotype Content Model and the BIAS Map," *Advances in Experimental Social Psychology* 40 (2008): 61–149; S. T. Fiske, "Stereotype Content: Warmth and Competence Endure," *Current Directions in Psychological Science* 27, no. 2 (2018): 67–73, https://doi.org/10.1177/0963721417738825.

3. Gordon Allport, *The Nature of Prejudice* (Doubleday, 1954).

4. Answer to quiz question #3.

5. Brittany M. Tausen, Katherine M. Douglass, Rebecca Hodges, Bella Rivera, and Caitlin Thomas, "Dining Against Dehumanization: A Mixed-Methods and Interdisciplinary Approach to Assessing the Humanizing Effects of Sharing a Meal with Individuals Experiencing Homelessness," *Journal of Psychology and Theology* 51, no. 2 (2022): 174–90, https://doi.org/10.1177/00916471221130325.

6. Tausen et al., "Dining Against Dehumanization."

7. Juliana Schroeder and Nicholas Epley, "Demeaning: Dehumanizing Others by Minimizing the Importance of Their Psychological Needs," *Journal of Personality and Social Psychology* 119, no. 4 (2020): 765–91, https://doi.org/10.1037/pspa0000199.

CHAPTER SEVEN

1. *U.S. News and World Report*, October 27, 1986.

2. Brittany M. Tausen, Jamie H. Lee, Anna S. Dischinger, and Isabelle A. Dennis, "When Dehumanization Does (and Does Not) Matter: Exploring the Relationship Between Social Justice, Avoidant Behaviors, and Intentions to Help Individuals Experiencing Homelessness," *Journal of Applied Social Psychology* (2023), https://doi.org/10.1111/jasp.12971.

3. Answer to quiz question #8.

4. John M. Gottman, *The Science of Trust: Emotional Attunement for Couples* (W. W. Norton, 2011).

CHAPTER EIGHT

1. Unlike for White immigrants, there was no path to citizenship or naturalization for Asian immigrants at the time. For more information, we would recommend the book *Welcoming the Stranger: Justice, Compassion and Truth in the Immigration Debate* by Matthew Soerens and Jenny Hwang Yang (InterVarsity Press, 2009). Drawing upon their experiences with the nonprofit organization World Relief, Soerens and Yang helpfully unpack the long and complicated history of immigration in the United States, including how it affects policy to this day.

2. See Mark Charles and Soong-Chan Rah, *Unsettling Truths: The Ongoing, Dehumanizing Legacy of the Doctrine of Discovery* (InterVarsity Press, 2019).

3. World Relief, a Christian organization that supports immigrants and refugees based on biblical principles like those found in Matt. 25:35, has done a great job addressing common myths about immigration. You can read about the top five myths here: "The Top 5 Immigration Myths Debunked," August 21, 2024, https://tinyurl.com/mv9dhb8m.

4. Muzafer Sherif, O. J. Harvey, B. Jack White, William R. Hood, and Carolyn W. Sherif, *Intergroup Conflict and Cooperation: The Robbers Cave Experiment* (University Book Exchange, 1961), 111. Italics in the original.

5. Michael M. Berkebile-Weinberg, Amy R. Krosch, and David M. Amodio, "Economic Scarcity Increases Racial Stereotyping in Beliefs and Face Representation," *Journal of Experimental Social Psychology* 102 (2022), https://doi.org/10.1016/j.jesp.2022.104354.

6. None of the participants in the study identified as Black; 91 percent identified as exclusively White.

7. Dr. Brenda Salter McNeil, "A Mindset of Abundance," sermon

preached at Quest Church, Seattle, WA, August 11, 2024, https://tinyurl.com/3zycajtv.

CHAPTER NINE

1. Nicholas Epley, *Mindwise: Why We Misunderstand What Others Think, Believe, Feel, and Want* (Vintage Books, 2014).

2. This saying may be based on David W. Augsburger's comment, "Being heard is so close to being loved that for the average person they are almost indistinguishable." In *Caring Enough to Hear and Be Heard: How to Hear and How to Be Heard in Equal Communication* (Baker, 1982).

3. John Calvin, *Institutes of the Christian Religion* 1.11.1–10, 2 vols. (Westminster, 1960), 1:99–111.

4. Ludwig Feuerbach, *The Essence of Christianity* (1957; reprint, Wipf & Stock, 2003), 31.

5. Anne Lamott, *Bird by Bird: Some Instructions on Writing and Life* (Vintage, 1995), 38.

CHAPTER TEN

1. Nancy M. Steblay, "Helping Behavior in Rural and Urban Environments: A Meta-analysis," *Psychological Bulletin* 102, no. 3 (1987): 346.

2. Shigehiro Oishi, Alexander J. Rothman, Mark Snyder, Jenny Su, Keri Zehm, Andrew W. Hertel, Marti Hope Gonzales, and Gary D. Sherman, "The Socioecological Model of Procommunity Action: The Benefits of Residential Stability," *Journal of Personality and Social Psychology* 93, no. 5 (2007): 831.

3. Adam Chandler, "Why Do Americans Move So Much More Than Europeans?," *Atlantic*, October 21, 2016, https://tinyurl.com/4wjzpmdd.

CHAPTER ELEVEN

1. Jamil Zaki, *The War for Kindness: Building Empathy in a Fractured World* (Crown, 2019).

2. Answer to quiz question #1.

3. Answer to quiz question #6. See L. Galen, R. Gore, and F. L. Shults, "Modeling the Effects of Religious Belief and Affiliation on Prosociality," *Secularism and Nonreligion* 10, no. 6 (2021): 1–21, https://

doi.org/10.5334/ snr.128; Luke W. Galen, Michael Sharp, and Alison McNulty, "Nonreligious Group Factors Versus Religious Belief in the Prediction of Prosociality," *Social Indicators Research* 122 (2015): 411–32.

CHAPTER TWELVE

1. Nicholas Epley and Juliana Schroeder, "Mistakenly Seeking Solitude," *Journal of Experimental Psychology: General* 143, no. 5 (2014): 1980.

2. Juliana Schroeder, "How to Fight Loneliness: Everyday Hacks for a Connected Life," Ted Talk, October 2023, https://tinyurl.com/4ahv335k.

3. Diana I. Tamir and Jason P. Mitchell, "Disclosing Information About the Self Is Intrinsically Rewarding," *Proceedings of the National Academy of Sciences* 109, no. 21 (2012): 8038–43.

4. Simone Weil, *Waiting for God* (Harper, 1951), 64.

5. Delores Williams, "A Womanist Perspective on Sin," in *A Troubling in My Soul: Womanist Perspectives on Evil and Suffering*, ed. Emilie Townes (Orbis, 2015), 130–49.

CHAPTER THIRTEEN

1. Fun fact: Psychology and neuroscience are inherently intertwined. Several PhD programs co-train in disciplines like social, cognitive, or affective psychology and neuroscience. In many universities, neuroscience departments are actually part of the psychology program rather than biology or medical programs.

2. Stephanie Cacioppo, *Wired for Love: A Neuroscientist's Journey Through Romance, Loss, and the Essence of Human Connection* (Flatiron Books, 2022).

3. Keyne Law, Lunch & Learn 2024 Guest Speaker, Faith Formation Project Podcast, https://tinyurl.com/pzv7djyz.

4. The National Alliance on Mental Illness (NAMI) has some practical resources to help you prepare for how to talk to someone who you think might be struggling with suicidal ideation. You can find one of their most relevant webpages here: https://www.nami.org/relationships/how-to-talk-and-listen-to-someone-experiencing-suicidal-thoughts (https://tinyurl.com/mrxfr45a).

CHAPTER FOURTEEN

1. N. Kteily, G. Hodson, and E. Bruneau, "They See Us as Less Than Human: Metadehumanization Predicts Intergroup Conflict via Reciprocal Dehumanization," *Journal of Personality and Social Psychology* 110 (2016): 343–70, https://doi.org/10.1037/pspa0000044.

2. The scale itself is a visual depiction of the "ascent of man" with the far left being represented by an ape walking on all fours and the far right, an image of a human walking upright. Participants slide a bar along a line to indicate where their own and other groups lie on the continuum.

3. Dominique DuBois Gilliard, Spring Summit 2024 keynote speaker, Faith Formation Project podcast, https://tinyurl.com/4hhc2hkr.

4. Karl Barth, *Church Dogmatics*, vol. III, part 2, *The Doctrine of Creation*, trans. H. Knight, G. W. Bromiley, J. K. S. Reid, and R. H. Fuller, ed. G. W. Bromiley and T. F. Torrance (T. & T. Clark, 1960). This wildly influential theologian shares his name's pronunciation with a character from *The Simpsons*.

5. Bob Dalton, *Everybody Is Somebody*, illustrated by Ritchie Collins (Sackcloth and Ashes, 2020); see also everyoneissomeone.com.